Praise for

YOU'RE 18! NOW WHAT?

"This is the book that I wish I had when I was starting out as a young adult. The book reads honestly, as if a good friend were offering advice on the aspects of our life that will have the greatest compounding impact. Had someone offered this book to me when I was in school, it could have saved me from learning these valuable lessons the hard way. Though we have had some of these financial conversations with our children, the material that Dr. Gilstein offers is more substantive and detailed. This book will provide needed guidance for years to come for anyone who reads it."

—**CATHY LOCKYER MOULTON**, president, Thomas Wynne, L.P. and MSH Ventures, L.P.

"There are so many young adulting issues covered, all of which give this mamma agita whenever I think about them and how I'm going to be helping my kids through these financial steps in life! As a librarian, I firmly believe that knowledge is power, and it's also a good way to reduce anxiety. This book is a fantastic tool to help with that—for parents and their kids."

—**LIZ FARLEY**, college librarian

"This book is a simple step-by-step of how to manage your finances as a young adult. It is written in a way that I find relatable as someone in this age range beginning my financial career. The credit chapter was extremely helpful, as I opened a credit card right when I turned 18. *You're 18! Now What?* has helped me understand many adult concepts that aren't so cut-and-dried, things that I never would have thought affected me at my young age."

—**SARAH GERBINO**, student, Penn State University

"The author provides practical advice with actionable steps for improving financial literacy and achieving financial goals throughout the book. Real-life examples and scenarios make the content relatable and applicable to young readers' lives. As a business major, I can confidently say that reading this book will without a doubt improve your understanding of money, financial responsibility, and reprogram your mind for a more financially successful future."

—**KYLE FASOLAK**, student, Coastal Carolina University

YOU'RE 18! NOW WHAT?

MASCOT BOOKS

www.mascotbooks.com

*You're 18! Now What?: A New Adult's Guide to Credit, Insurance, Investing, Job Searches, and Other Real-World Sh*t*

The information in this book is general in nature and not intended for specific, individualized tax, legal, or investment advice. Where specific advice is necessary or appropriate, please consult with a qualified tax advisor, certified public accountant, financial planner, or investment manager.

The discussion of various investment types throughout this book is in no way intended as a solicitation for any product or service. Investing involves risk, including possible loss of principal. Investment and insurance products are not deposits, are not FDIC-insured, are not insured by any government agency, are not guaranteed by a bank or any affiliate of a bank, and may lose value.

Much of the information here is based on tax year 2023. Please consider how potential changes to the tax code in future years might affect your planning.

This work is sold with the understanding that neither the author nor the publisher is held responsible for the results accrued from the advice in this book.

For more information, please contact:
Mascot Books, an imprint of Amplify Publishing Group
620 Herndon Parkway, Suite 220
Herndon, VA 20170
info@mascotbooks.com

Library of Congress Control Number: 2024903928

CPSIA Code: PRV0524A

ISBN-13: 979-8-89138-100-1

Printed in the United States

For Stephanie, Brittany, Shaina, and Jake

You are my heart!

Remember that there is nothing you cannot do!

And to my students, "Be invaluable for what you share—not what you know."

YOU'RE 18! NOW WHAT?

A NEW ADULT'S GUIDE TO

CREDIT, INSURANCE, INVESTING, JOB SEARCHES, AND OTHER REAL-WORLD SH*T

Catherine Gilstein

MASCOT BOOKS

Contents

PREFACE

This book is about empowering students and young adults with knowledge about financial literacy, understanding their relationship with money, and how to navigate lifelong skills such as applying for a job, getting an apartment, opening a bank account, and other day-to-day needs.

Although there are books about finance and investing, students and young adults want to know about the basics of money *before* investing. What do you do when you get to college and you are suddenly on your own with all the freedoms you thought you wanted, but you don't know how to prepare for when you are finished with school? The contents of *You're 18! Now What?* encompass a basic relationship with money that goes deeper, including how to navigate a job hunt, insurance, taxes, and other information that is valuable to this age group beyond strictly finance.

The pages within this book are about discovery and answering questions that students and young adults have in a simple way so that you can be empowered to make sound decisions with a little bit of guidance. The target market for this book is sixteen- to twenty-four-year-olds. This book is also a great reference to look back at when you are a bit older if you are moving out on your own for the first time at age twenty-six, twenty-seven, or later. The topics I cover represent key milestones in people's lives that if not known can be difficult to manage and navigate alone. This book can also be presented to parents of children who are approaching college or moving out to give those parents a sense of relief that there is a resource to help empower their grown or nearly grown children with knowledge and clear decision-making. It is my hope that this book will be a staple in people's homes, college campuses, and high schools throughout the country.

I have spent a significant amount of time in retail banking helping people obtain loans, investments, annuities, and insurance. I have also spent the last ten years as a college professor teaching economics, management of human resources, marketing, operations management, consumer behavior, and other business courses to undergraduate students. I have used my knowledge from my corporate positions and academia to bring both theory and practice of real-life scenarios into the classroom, which gives students the perspective of seeing how the courses they are taking now will be relevant to them once they graduate.

You're 18! Now What? will empower high school and college students and other young adults to conquer the ins and outs of navigating basic financial and life skills that are not taught but need to be known. There are so many topics that are discussed in day-to-day engagements and so many questions that students have. With the information provided in these pages, students will be encouraged to learn more, do more, and take ownership of what you can control. Knowing about finances, buying a car, moving into your own apartment, or just doing laundry can be overwhelming—especially if you must learn it all at the same time. Within this book, we tackle the easy, difficult, and sometimes mundane tasks that need to be addressed and simplify them for students and young adults so you can be confident and successful in whatever endeavors you pursue.

PROLOGUE

So much pressure.

So much emphasis.

Years and years of competitions, tests, comparing ourselves to our peers in and out of the classrooms. And why?

If only I could tell my younger self. If only I could have been present in that moment. Maybe it would have been different. Maybe I could have seen the signs. And maybe, just maybe, it would be easier right now.

How is it that I don't know what to do? How is it that I don't know who to call? How is it that I just don't know? Was I not paying attention? Did I miss it? Does everyone else know except for me? This can't be! Not just for me, but for everyone else as well. I ask questions. I get blank stares. Why didn't anyone tell me? Why wasn't it important? Why does it have to be so difficult now?

So many questions. I hope I can get through it. Someone must know how to navigate all of this. Now I can!

Chapter 1

I CAN . . . KNOW MY RELATIONSHIP WITH MONEY

Can money buy happiness? I don't think so, but it can help with what you need, what you want, and where you want to go. The biggest thing is not to overcomplicate it. We have a certain amount of money that we can spend and a certain number of obligations that need to be paid. What is left over are what I refer to as "fun self" and "future self." What do you want for fun that you are not willing to give up—maybe that fancy coffee once a week? Have that and don't feel guilty about it. What do you want for your future? This is where you can see what you are willing to give up in order to get that.

Needs, wants, future self.

Money is such an important part of our lives, but no one wants to talk about it. The important piece is that you can continually learn more about money. Money, in and of itself, is not a resource. From an economic perspective, money allows you to purchase resources, which are land, labor, capital (not financial capital), and entrepreneurship—what do you want to own? What is good or bad about money? What should you know about money? Why is money such a difficult topic to understand? This chapter clears up a few things about money including credit, banking institutions, debt, and budgets, to name a few.

CREDIT SCORE

Let's start with the most important thing that you can own, and it is not your house or your condo or your car or your laptop or your phone—it is your credit score. The range for a credit score is from 300 to 850. Credit allows you to purchase things now and pay for them later.

Without a good credit score, you cannot secure an apartment, house, car—or even sometimes a job. Why it is important? A credit score is a measure of a person's credit worthiness or trustworthiness and lets the lender know if they will pay back what they borrow. The higher the score, the better chance of securing a loan or borrowing money. A person's social security number is connected to their credit score. The more creditworthy the individual (or business), the more reliable or trustworthy that individual (or business) is said to be. So how do you build credit? My suggestion is to obtain a credit card. You can accomplish this by being added to a credit card that your parent, guardian, or older sibling has so you can become an authorized user and additional owner on their account. Once this is established, you can start to build a credit file for yourself. Perhaps you can use the card for gas in your car and then pay that amount each month the card is due. Another option is to obtain a secure credit card. This is where you apply for a credit card and if they give you a $300 line of credit, you send the credit card company $300. This way, you are using the money that you initially put onto the card, which is no risk to the credit card company because you will have "secured" the card with a specified amount. Once you have had either of these for about a year and are using and paying the card off each month, you will have established credit for yourself and can begin to get credit in your own name.

It is also important to note that you are entitled to one free credit report each year at annualcreditreport.com. Please note that freecreditreport.com is not entirely free. There are three reporting agencies for credit, which are TransUnion, Equifax, and Experian, and they report what you are charging and what you are paying each month. These reporting agencies determine your creditworthiness. It is a good idea to get your personalized report from each one. It is worthwhile to check your report each year to make sure there are no errors or misinformation on your report. If there are errors, you can file a dispute with the reporting agency that has the error.

Check your report

with a reputable agency at annualcreditreport.com.

Example:

Suppose you want to buy a home for $200,000, a modest purchase relative to the median price for new homes sold nationwide. You sign up for a thirty-year fixed-rate mortgage and put down a 5 percent deposit on the home, which is $10,000. You are now taking out a mortgage for $190,000 over thirty years.

If your credit score were 760 or 770 (which would be in the "very good" category), here's an estimate of what you'd pay:

- 7.74 percent APR
- $1,864.04 monthly payment
- $299,553.39 total interest over your mortgage term

On the other hand, if you had just "fair" credit with a score of 680, your terms would be less appealing. An estimate of what you would pay would look like this:

- 8.33 percent APR
- $1,942.27 monthly payment
- $327,718.28 total interest over your mortgage term

If your credit score is 640 (which would be considered "poor"), you'd be looking at the following:

- 8.76 percent APR
- $2,000.25 monthly payment
- $348,591.67 total interest over your mortgage term

In these examples, the better score would save you **nearly $50,000 over the life of the loan.** The difference between a score of 699 and 700 is the difference between a "fair" credit rating and a "good" credit rating. With numbers like these, there's no denying the importance of your credit score range.*

---

* The numbers represented here are from mortgagecalculator.org as of November 1, 2023.

Another important piece of credit is how your credit score is determined. It is a mix of a few different factors—35 percent is based on your payment history (on time payments or late payments); 30 percent is utilization of credit (how much credit you are using—it is recommended to use less than 30 percent of the total credit line); 15 percent is length of credit (how long you have had a credit card—which takes into consideration the youngest and oldest account and the average age of all of your accounts); 10 percent is a mix of credit (mortgage, car, department store card, credit/debit card—good debt and bad debt); and 10 percent is new credit (meaning when was the last time you opened a new line of credit).

CREDIT CARDS AND DEBIT CARDS

The biggest misconception I see students and young adults struggling with is the difference between a credit card and a debit card. A credit card is issued by a company, and you are given a specific monetary amount limit to spend on that card. You use the card and must pay it back each month. If you use the card and only pay a portion back (minimum amount due), then you are subject to accruing interest on that card until the balance is paid off. For example, if you have a limit of $500, then you are authorized to charge $500 on that card. If you charge $300 on the card, then there might be a minimum amount due of $25 for that month. If you pay only the minimum amount due, then you are charged interest and the next month you have only $200 left to charge on the card. The $500 limit is the maximum you can charge, and that amount is not reset to zero unless the full amount is paid each month.

A debit card is a card that is linked to your bank account. Once you use the card, the amount is debited from your bank account balance almost immediately. If there is no money in your account, you cannot use the debit card to purchase anything. You must deposit more money into your bank account to use your debit card to purchase something.

BANKS, ONLINE BANKS, AND CREDIT UNIONS

There are different institutions where you can keep your money. We are not talking about investing just yet—we will get to that later. Where do you prefer to keep your checking account and savings account? It is a matter of personal preference. I like a physical bank where I can go in and talk to someone if I want to open an additional account or learn about a new savings tool they offer. I also like the convenience of an online bank where I can just automatically transfer money into it and gain a higher interest rate on my savings account because the overhead costs are lower for this type of institution.

> **How to tell the difference?**
>
> **Credit is borrowing and debit is directly taken out of your account at the time of purchase.**
>
> **Check your account BEFORE you buy.**
>
> **A good way to remember it is like this:**
>
> **Credit=Borrow, so Credit=Can I borrow?**
>
> **Debit=Direct, so Debit=Deleted now!**

There are also credit unions where you can keep your money, though you must be part of that group to use them. Examples are the Police & Fire Credit Union—you must be police or fire personnel (or a relative of) to be able to use this credit union. Typically, credit unions will have a lower interest rate for car loans than a private bank will. I suggest shopping around for rates on everything where your money is concerned. Bankrate.com is a great resource.

SAVINGS

What I like to say is that if you can control your saving now, you can control your savings later in life. What you have is time on your side to save money. There is a 50/30/20 rule when it comes to money: 50 percent for needs, 30 percent for wants, 20 percent for savings (or future you). As a young adult, you have the opportunity to save much more than 20 percent of your income. My rule of thumb for a young adult when you are working part-time and still living at home rent-free is that it is a good idea to save half and spend half. If you do this on a consistent basis, you will have accumulated more savings than you can imagine. Putting your money into a high-rate savings account is a great idea because with a regular checking account, the interest earned is about 0.01 percent annual percentage rate (APR). With a high-yield savings account, you can earn about 4.50 percent APR or more. As of this writing, Synchrony savings is paying 4.75 percent APR on their high-yield savings account. Most high-yield savings accounts require a minimum deposit. With Synchrony Bank, there is no minimum deposit, no minimum balance to maintain, and no monthly fee.

Synchrony Financial has its headquarters in Stamford, Connecticut. They are FDIC insured (Federal Deposit Insurance Corporation), which is an independent agency created by Congress to maintain stability and public confidence in the nation's financial system. The FDIC insures deposits up to $250,000 per depositor, per insured bank, for each ownership category. Every little bit of savings adds up so consistent savings, even if a small amount, will accumulate over time. A budget is helpful to keep track of your spending habits so that you can work toward your needs, wants, and future-you savings.

SIMPLE INTEREST AND COMPOUND INTEREST

Interest is money that is earned on your money. There is simple interest and compound interest. Simple interest (calculated as Principal x Rate x Time) is compensation from the bank when you deposit your funds, and they lend out your money. The financial institution will give you something called simple interest (a fixed rate amount). Compound interest (table and formula below), on the other hand, is where you earn interest not only on your initial investment but also on the accumulated interest over time. It's like a snowball effect, growing bigger and bigger as time goes by. The earlier you start, the more powerful this snowball effect becomes. The principal amount of money you have is multiplied by the interest rate that is offered by the savings institution, and that amount is continually compounded to add to your savings. This is compound interest. As an early saver, you have time and compounding interest on your side to begin to build wealth. Thecalculatorsite.com is a great resource for figuring out and explaining calculations.

Check out the end of the book or youre18nowwhat.com or just use this QR code for the 50/30/20 spreadsheet and other budget-friendly checkups.

The rule of 72 (DelVecchio & Jacobs, 2016) is a quick way to figure out how long it will take you to double your money once you put it into your high-yield savings account. Deposit it into your banking institution. If you divide 72 by the interest rate you are receiving, that will give you the number of years it will take to see your money double:

Do you know the rule of 72?

72 / 6% = 12 years to double your money
or
72 / 8% = 9 years to double your money

SIMPLE INTEREST	COMPOUND INTEREST
Levied only on the loan amount or principal.	Levied on the loan amount as well as on its interest.
A small percentage of the principal as agreed between lender and borrower.	A small percentage of principal and amassed simple interest as agreed between lender and borrower
Steady wealth growth.	Wealth growth increases at a higher pace due to compounding.
Lower returns compared to compound interest.	Higher returns compared to simple interest.
Wealth accumulation will be at a lower rate.	Wealth accumulation will be at a faster rate.

GOOD DEBT AND BAD DEBT

Believe it: there are two kinds of debt—good debt and bad debt. If you can control your debt now, you can control your debt later in life. Bad debt is credit card debt that spirals out of control, such as when you are using your card and not paying the full balance on it, so you are being charged interest on the outstanding money owed to the credit card company. This can snowball very quickly. Good debt is when you are using credit to show your trustworthiness with credit, such as by owning or leasing a car; using a credit card for a large purchase and having a promotional zero percent interest rate for 12 or 18 months while you pay it off; or purchasing some type of home (single family, multifamily, condo, townhouse, etc.).

For the math geek who wants to calculate on their own.

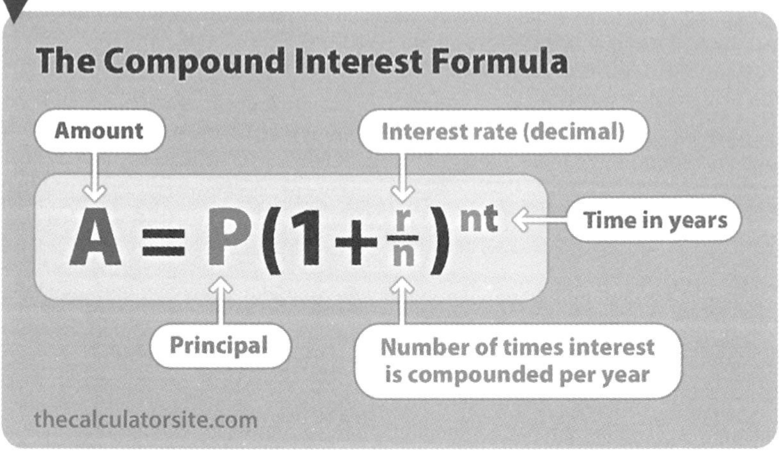

INCOME AND WEALTH

Income is what you earn weekly, monthly, or yearly. Your income is not your take-home pay; your income is your gross (total) earnings.

Your take-home pay is also called your net pay (after taxes, medical, dental, retirement, or whatever else you have automatically deducted). Wealth is what you accumulate over time. I find that people have no problem saving for the immediate but have trouble saving for the future. It can be hard to imagine saving for retirement when you are so young. Starting small and creating a habit of saving each time you earn money, no matter how little, will add up over time. Putting money away in different "buckets" (we will cover this in greater detail later) is how wealth is built.

If you have a job that pays salary plus commission, spend your salary, save your commission. If you have a job that pays salary plus tips, spend your salary, save your tips. These little habits build upon each other and add to your overall wealth and financial security.

If you can save for the weekend trip now, you will have savings for your future self. If you can control your debt early on, you can control your debt in the future. If you can earn income now, you can build wealth for your future.

Save now → savings later
Debt now → debt later
Income now → wealth later

BUDGETING

A budget can be monotonous when you begin, but like anything, it takes time to build a habit; when you start now with a budget, you will have control over it for the rest of your life. Budgeting is helpful because it lets you see what you are earning versus what you are spending and know exactly what you are spending your money on. With a debit card, you just swipe, swipe, swipe, and have no idea where your money is going.

Are you spending your money on needs, wants, or savings (future you)? Are you spending on food, travel, or shopping? It is a good idea

Remember, debit = direct payment NOW.

to keep a tally of where your spending habits are so you can see your trends. Do you spend more when out with other people? Do you shop online when you are bored? Knowing your spending patterns and habits can keep you focused on what is important to you—needs, wants, or savings (future you). Recall the savings section and the 50/30/20 rule when it comes to money: 50 percent for needs, 30 percent for wants, 20 percent for savings (or future you). With a little practice, you will be able to control your spending habits.

Chapter 2

I CAN . . . FINANCE MY EDUCATION

As I think back to when I when I was in high school and contemplating my next steps, it was frightening to imagine how I would be able to pay for school. I knew that I wanted a four-year degree and wanted to major in accounting. Within one semester of attending college, I switched my major to finance and management to give me a wider scope of job opportunities for further down the road in my career. I never regretted that decision, and I utilized every person in the guidance office of my high school to figure out what to do to pay for school for myself. I was lucky to obtain scholarships and loans and went to a local city university of New York (CUNY—Brooklyn College). I knew I didn't want to be far from home and wanted to commute so that I could work part-time in my local community.

I worked as a part-time bank teller while in school and learned so much about the banking and financial industry and knew the choice I made was the right one for me. I happened to spend more than twenty years in the banking, finance, and insurance industries and then went on to academia where I teach both undergraduate and graduate students different business courses. Although I was not in the same industry, I didn't stray far from the finance space. What's important is finding something that you enjoy and working in that field. And no, you do not have to have it all figured out right now. Some take years to do that, and that is perfectly okay too.

Thinking about furthering your education and not knowing which direction you are headed in can be overwhelming. Adding to that, wondering how you are going to pay for it just creates another layer of uncertainty. Know that there are options for everyone in financing their education, but you need to take ownership of it.

TWO-YEAR OR FOUR-YEAR DEGREE OR TRADE SCHOOL

Now that you have finished high school, now what? So many people will ask: where are you going? What are you doing? First, let me say that you do not need to know the answers just yet. There are plenty of people who start their dreams later in life. What is important is to have some kind of path. A four-year degree is not for everyone.

School—Dollars—Eeek!

If you know that you want to go into the medical field, lawyer tract, or psychology services, then it is a good idea to get a four-year degree. You will have to further your education beyond a bachelor's degree to be a doctor, a lawyer, or a psychologist.

There are some students who are unsure of the path they want. Choosing a two-year, or associate degree, is a smart and economical choice here. You can attend a community college and take different general education classes to see what you like, what you don't like, what is enjoyable, what is fun, and where your passion is. It is true that when you are doing something you love, it is never work. This can give you an opportunity to see if you want to further your education and then transfer to a four-year college or university. There is nothing wrong with having options.

Maybe you know that you love doing electrical work or plumbing work. Choosing a trade school is a great option and can lead to a great career. There are plenty of community colleges that offer trade school options, so there is some research to be done. There are also some high schools that have agreements with trade schools where you can take both high school courses and trade courses, or both high school and community college courses.

LOANS AND GRANTS

Now that you have decided which path to take for furthering your education beyond high school, let us look at different options for how you will be able to pay for school. Obtaining loans and grants for school can be tricky. Let's start with the main difference—loans must be paid back, and grants are funds that are given to you and do not have to be paid back. It is a good idea to start with your high school and work with the guidance counselors to see what is available for you in terms of loans and grants. There are government loans, both subsidized and unsubsidized, that can be obtained. There are parent PLUS loans through the government, where your parent or guardian will obtain the loan for you. There are grants (free), which can be available depending upon your individual situation and the school you choose to go to.

SUBSIDIZED AND UNSUBSIDIZED

Most undergraduate students will receive both subsidized and unsubsidized loans, but a subsidized loan has an advantage because the interest payments are "subsidized" by the government and the interest does not accrue until you leave school. The interest rate is also a fixed rate, meaning that the rate will not change.

The Department of Education pays the interest on subsidized federal loans as long as the student is enrolled at least half-time, which is considered six credits hours; however, a student borrower can save money by making payments while still in school. Since no two people are alike or in the same financial situation, depending on the size of the loan and your income level, some can qualify for an income-driven

	Subsidized Loans	Unsubsidized Loans
Financial Need	based on financial need	does not require a financial need
Eligible Borrowers	undergraduate students	undergraduate or graduate students
Interest	fixed interest rate interest doesn't accrue until you leave school	fixed interest rate interest accrues from the time the loan is disbursed
Maximum Amounts	Total Aggregated Limit: $23,000	Undergraduate Students Total Aggregated Limit: $57,500 (inc. subsidized) Graduate Students Total Aggregated Limit: $138,500 (inc. subsidized)

repayment plan, ultimately reducing the monthly payments once the loan starts in repayment. Federalstudentaid.gov is a great resource for details on subsidized and unsubsidized loans, how much you can borrow, how to apply for the loan you need, how you will receive your loan, and the different repayment plan options that you have.

> You have to pay loans back! Grants are FREE!

The table on page 16 shows some details of subsidized and unsubsidized loans.

PARENT PLUS LOANS

A parent PLUS loan is a "federal loan that parents of dependent undergraduate students can use to help pay for college or career school."* The person applying for the PLUS loan must be the biological or adoptive parent (or stepparent) of the dependent undergraduate student who is enrolled at least half-time (six credit hours), must not have adverse credit (remember Chapter 1), and must meet the general requirements for obtaining federal student aid. The advantage of the PLUS loan is that the maximum amount that can be borrowed is the cost of attendance for the school that the student is attending minus any other financial awards the student receives.

EXAMPLE:	COST OF ATTENDANCE	$50,000 PER YEAR
	Other awards and grants	$15,000 per year
	PLUS, loan determined	$35,000 per year

* https://studentaid.gov/understand-aid/types/loans/plus/parent

Each year that the student attends school, the biological or adoptive parent (or stepparent) must apply for the PLUS loan. The same is true for other loans—each must be completed for each year. It is important to note that when obtaining a PLUS loan, your biological or adoptive parent (or stepparent) must ask for a deferment, or they will be expected to start paying it back as soon as the loan is paid out to the school. When they ask for a deferment, they will not be asked to make payments on the loan until six months after the student graduates—as long as you are enrolled half-time (six credit hours).

Another key for obtaining a PLUS loan is to ask for a bit more than you actually need, because they will take a fee off the top of the loan: "The loan fee is a percentage of the loan amount and is proportionately deducted from each loan disbursement. The percentage for all Direct PLUS loans first dispersed on or after October 1, 2020, is 4.228 percent."† If you need to borrow $35,000 for your fall and spring semesters, there will be a fee imposed (as shown in the chart below) and the total amount of money you will receive will be $33,520.20, leaving you short for the amount due to the school, and you will have to come up with the remaining amount out of pocket. If you plan on attending Summer classes, then you will need to apply separately for loans to cover those.

LOAN AMOUNT	FEE	AMOUNT DISPERSED
$35,000	4.228% ($1,479.80)	$33,520.20

† https://studentaid.gov

SCHOLARSHIPS

Scholarships are another option for obtaining "free" money to go to school. Scholarships are given out for written essays or based on company offerings. What I find is that most students don't apply for them. And let me repeat: this is free money. Some scholarships are a few hundred dollars, and some are a few thousand dollars. It is the same as I said about saving money—every little bit will accumulate. For scholarships, there is not a limit on how many essays you can write and how many different scholarships you can apply for, so a few hundred dollars here, and a few thousand dollars there, and you can have a sizable amount of money for school.

Aside from checking with your guidance office at school about companies that offer scholarships, you can also ask other people you know. There are corporations that are willing to give scholarships to the children, and sometimes even grandchildren, of the employees that work there—ask relatives if their company is one of the many that offer these.

> **If you don't apply, you don't receive.**
>
> **Who doesn't want FREE money for school?**

A good resource is The Scholarship Center, Inc.[‡] This website is constantly updated to reflect what scholarships are available, how to apply for them, and what the requirements are to obtain them. For example, they have awarded nearly $2,000,000 in scholarship money to qualified students in the United States through the Dunkin' Donuts Community Partnership and the Dunkin' Donuts Scholarship Fund.

‡ The Scholarship Center, Inc. is an online resource for locating thousands of scholarships for students throughout the United States.

> **Decisions, decisions?**
>
> Two-year degree
>
> Four-year degree
>
> Trade school
>
> Straight to work
>
> Trust that you will make the right choice for you!

For students who are enrolled in a community college already, there are still opportunities to get a scholarship. PepsiCo S.M.I.L.E. scholarships are granted to students who have completed their associate degree and are looking to transfer to a four-year school to earn their bachelor's degree. If you are headed to work before deciding if you want to pursue a degree, there are companies like Chick-Fil-A, Starbucks, and many others that offer scholarships or tuition programs for their employees. The important thing is to contact the relevant office to confirm qualifications for scholarships, requirements, transmission of documents, and deadlines. The worst thing is to forget the deadline, so keep a timeline for yourself to manage what scholarships you are applying to.

FURTHERING YOUR EDUCATION

When you look at the options for furthering your education, there are a few factors to consider aside from cost. Here we are looking at the cost-benefit analysis. What is the cost of furthering your education beyond a bachelor's degree and what are the benefits to you once you do so? In other words, is it worth it to pay for furthering your education if you cannot get the return on your money by securing a job that is going to cover the costs of what you have paid?

Obtaining a master's degree can be beneficial for some professions, but not for all. If you want to be a doctor, lawyer, psychologist, physician's assistant, therapist, etc., then you will need to further your education beyond a bachelor's degree. If, on the other hand, you would like to get an MBA or a master's in organizational leadership, then my suggestion to save money is to secure a job and work for a year or two—then you can have your company pay for your master's degree by using their tuition repayment program (a lot of companies offer this within their benefits package). Even an accountant does not need a master's degree. You can secure a job with a great accounting firm, gain some experience, have them sponsor you to sit for the CPA exam, and use the tuition reimbursement to get the thirty additional credits needed to sit for the exam and become a certified public accountant. You do not need to become a CPA unless you want to expand on your knowledge and distinguish yourself from other accountants. This option gives you the best of both worlds—by the time you finish the master's program of your choice, you will have both a degree and work experience (without the student debt) and will be able to advance your career to the next level.

Chapter 3

I CAN . . . LIVE ON MY OWN

Getting a first place to live is one of the most exciting things you can do for yourself. Not only are you saying, "I am an independent, strong person," but you are beginning to shape your future self. Take into consideration the location, your family size (if moving in with other people), your current debt, and any potential expenses such as utilities or lifestyle—maybe you enjoy a fancy coffee every day or a standard dinner out weekly with friends. All of this should be included in your budget for moving out. It can also be overwhelming trying to navigate a move, but no worries—I will walk you through the basics here, and you will be successful when your time comes.

Home sweet home—living on my own.

SECURING AN APARTMENT

Where are you going to live? Do you prefer the hustle of a city or the quietness of the suburbs? Do you prefer an apartment, condo, townhome, or house? Each one has its pros and cons. Living in or near a city can mean less commuting and saving money on that, but the cost of a city apartment can be higher. Living outside the city or in the suburbs can be a longer commute and may be more expensive, but the apartment itself may be less per month. It is a matter of preference, and this is where you start to shape your future self. By deciding on the place where you want to live, and the type of apartment you want, you are deciding on the lifestyle that you want to have at the moment. Any of this can change at any time and that is perfectly okay. You do not need to have it all figured out right now. No one does—needs change, desires change, jobs change, our lives change—and we grow with them constantly, reshaping ourselves all the time.

Let's think back to chapter 1 when credit was covered. Since your credit score is the most important thing you own, you need to have a decent credit score to secure an apartment. This is the other key piece to getting your own place, so make sure that your credit is in order, because most places will check your credit history to see if you are creditworthy to rent a place from them. You will also need to have a decent amount of savings on hand. Even if you have your friends for a moving party to move all your things, and you just have to feed them in return, you will still need a decent amount of cash on hand. To rent a typical place, you will need three months of rent up-front. Yes, three months! They will ask for one month up-front for a deposit, one month up-front for security (just in case you decide to bale), and one month of actual rent.

There are different ways to find your place, and www.apartments.com is a great resource. You can search locally for an apartment, condo, townhome, or home to rent. There is a rental calculator that you can use to help with the budget and a simple budget spreadsheet in the appendices as well. The rental calculator uses the 50/30/20 rule that was covered in the savings section of chapter one—spending 50 percent on living expenses (needs), 30 percent on daily expenses (wants), and 20 percent on savings (future you). Most landlords (the people you will be renting from) ask that no more than 30 percent of your take-home (after-tax) income is spent on rent. We all know that what you make is not the same as what you take home, and we will go deeper into this in chapter 8 when we cover your paycheck and taxes. This will mean getting a place you love and knowing that you will be able to afford it on a long-term basis and set yourself up for success. Don't fear—there is an apartment to-do list and an apartment necessities checklist for you (located in the supplemental materials section).

UTILITIES AND NECESSITIES

What utilities will you need to cover when you get your own place? What necessities will you have to purchase? The utilities to add into your budget include electric and/or gas, and possibly water and sewer depending on where you choose to live. If you are renting a house, you might be required to pay for lawn maintenance for the property, which can be costly. It never hurts to ask too many questions when you are paying for something. Use a checklist (listed in supplemental materials) to make sure you have covered everything. There are some apartment complexes that put everything together for you, and your utilities will be included in the rental payment and listed as a separate line-item number on your monthly invoice for rent. Other places you live, you will have to contact the electric company to have the electric turned on. Same thing for the gas company and the cable and internet companies. For the cable and internet companies to start service at your new place takes some time, and a credit check will be done. While electric and gas can just be turned on by the company, the cable and internet companies will have to come out to your new place and get it set up. You have to pick a time that is convenient for you, and you might have to miss a day of work to get that set up. Wasn't it great when your parents took care of this for you?

Another expense could be your cell phone bill. Perhaps, you will no longer be part of a family coverage plan and might have to get a cell phone in your name. You can contact the cell phone company directly and ask to have your phone moved to your name. This is another place where your credit score might be checked.

The expense that I see go most overlooked is the cost of stocking your home with stuff. The stuff I am talking about includes the cost to stock a bathroom. Once you start adding up the cost of Tylenol, cold and flu medication, toothpaste, toilet paper, shampoo, conditioner, and other necessities, the cost of stocking one bathroom can be several hundred dollars. A good rule of thumb is to buy a replacement item when the last one is put out to be used. There is not going to be a bathroom fairy that comes in and stocks up on all the things that are running low—it is now part of your responsibility.

Check out the necessities sheet at the end of the book or at youre18nowwhat.com or just use this QR code.

When furnishing your first apartment, try not to buy everything all at once. Get into the space and see how it feels. Purchase your bed and a sofa and then take a step back. Really think about the space, incorporate your style, and use your budget. Stores like Target, Ikea, and Wayfair go a long way.

INSURANCE

Insurance for a person moving out on their own for the first time can be a bit tricky. Why do you need insurance? You are just renting an apartment, right? Wrong! Let's start with what insurance is. Insurance is something that we purchase to hedge against a risk of loss or harm. We purchase auto insurance in case we get into a car accident. The same holds true here—we purchase, in this case, renter's insurance (because we are renting a space) just in case something should be lost, stolen, or damaged. With renter's insurance, you will pay a premium (either monthly or yearly) and if something should happen, you will receive a monetary benefit from your loss.

Renter's insurance is relatively inexpensive, and many landlords and apartment companies will ask you to have insurance when you move into the property. You will pay what is called a premium—either monthly, quarterly, or annually—to protect your things from loss or damage. According to the 2021 data from Progressive Home Renters, the average cost in the United States (excluding Alaska and Hawaii) is $14–$30 per month for about $30,000 worth of belongings in the home.

There are several factors that make up this number, which include location, type of residence, coverage selection, and some states include an insurance score based upon your credit report and loss history. Loss history is considered when you have had coverage in your name before and have reported a loss or damage of items in your home. The more reports you make, the higher the premium you will be paying.

SAVING FOR A HOUSE

So now that you have your first apartment, how do you begin to start saving for a house? For one, following the 50/30/20 rule is great. If you can keep to your budget by remembering to pay yourself first, you will build up a nice savings over time. For first-time homeowners,

> Here's that 50/30/20 rule again.

there are programs available for as little as 3.5 percent down payment on a home.

Paying 20 percent down is ideal because you avoid paying private mortgage insurance (PMI), which is a cost included in your payment when you put down less than 20 percent on a home purchase. PMI costs can range from 0.22 percent to 2.25 percent of your mortgage. How much you pay in PMI is dependent upon the total loan amount, so the higher the loan, the higher the PMI payment.

PMI is also dependent upon your credit score—yes, your credit score again—so the higher the credit score, the lower the PMI percentage. It is best to calculate the low end (0.22 percent) and the high end (2.25 percent) to determine what your PMI will be, or you can ask your lender for your precise percentage.

The positive side is that even if you put down less than 20 percent on your first home, you can stop paying the PMI portion once your loan-to-value (LTV) ratio is below 80 percent. Lenders will use an amortization schedule to determine when that time is and typically eliminate the PMI when you reach a 78 percent LTV. To calculate your LTV on your own, you can divide the loan amount by the property value—what the home is appraised at—and then multiply that number by 100 to get the percentage. If the result is 80 percent or lower, you qualify to have your PMI payment removed. Keep an eye on this yourself and check it about two to two and a half years into your mortgage payments. The lender will not notify you to have the PMI removed—this is something you will need to request.

Most people take out a thirty-year mortgage, which is standard. Some people like to take out a fifteen-year mortgage because the thought of thirty years seems overwhelming. A fifteen-year mortgage will be more costly, but the home will be paid off in half the time. My rule is to take the thirty-year mortgage and make extra payments to lower the life of the loan.

On average, if you make biweekly payments every month or make just one extra payment a year on the mortgage, you will take about seven to eight years off the life of the loan. This would cut your mortgage to twenty-two or twenty-three years instead of thirty, and you would not have to worry about the higher monthly payment of a fifteen-year mortgage.

Fifteen-year mortgage!
Thirty-year mortgage!
Refinance options!
Research them all!

Some people have a high interest rate on their mortgage and after a few years, they refinance the mortgage at the lower interest rate to reduce their payments. Sometimes that is not the wise choice, especially if you must pay points to get the lower rate. This is something to speak with your lender about since there are many factors that go into a refinance for a home.

Chapter 4

I CAN . . . FIND THE PERFECT JOB

During the recession of 2008–2009, I found myself laid off with all the other middle managers across the country. I was not in school. I did not live at home. I had my own family that needed my income. I was panicked. I searched online for jobs for days. Without success, I thought it would be the perfect time to get my MBA. I enrolled in night school and thought, why not work in retail? I went on the Bloomingdale's website, applied for a job, and could not upload any information—not my résumé, my experience, nothing.

It was extremely frustrating. The next day I put my two younger children in the car and drove to Bloomingdale's. I walked into the human resources office with my résumé and children in tow. I explained to the receptionist my struggles with the website and gave my résumé to her. After looking it over for a few minutes, she asked for my email address to send me the direct link for the application process and the hiring manager. Within a week, I had a job.

> Sometimes you need to go out of your comfort zone.

Sometimes you need to think outside the box and just grab your kids and go. I had that job throughout my master's program and then continued working there part-time for years because of the people and the respect that I was given when I needed a job the most.

So how do you go about finding a job? Finished with school and ready to work—sounds great, but you will have to work a long time, so take your time finding a spot. While you are in school, there might be opportunities to work part-time or secure an internship. These are the best positions to get because they can give insight into what you like and what you don't like in a job or a company.

Most colleges have a career development center that will assist in writing your résumé, doing a mock interview, and practice for presentations. Some schools even have some type of career closet where you can access a professional wardrobe to use in the interview process. Many students do not realize the amenities on campus aside from the dining hall. Use the resources to your advantage. Every resource is an opportunity for personal growth.

SEARCH

So how do you begin a search for a job? Reach out to the career development center at your school and sign up for Handshake.* The process is simple:

* Handshake—a platform for students to build the career they want—no matter where they are from or what school they attend.

1. sign up and download the app to your phone;
2. create a profile for yourself and get personalized job recommendations;
3. meet with employers to learn about the company culture and open roles;
4. apply and secure the job.

The best thing about Handshake is that schools have screened the employers so that students know they are going to be with a solid company that cares about the future generation securing jobs.

What if you are not attending school? Where do you begin to find a job? My suggestion is to create a LinkedIn[†] profile and start building your professional image. You can add your skills and interests and connect to people that share your professional passions. Who do you know in the tech space, or the banking industry, or the restaurant space? You can follow a person or a company. If you know the companies that interest you, follow them and check for hiring opportunities. If you are seeking an opportunity, you can add the #Open to Work feature on your profile which allows your network and the LinkedIn community to know that you are looking for a job. LinkedIn is a free social media platform so there is no cost involved. Let me repeat: free!

So, no matter if you are in school or out, there are free opportunities available to you for finding a job, but you need to take accountability and reach out. No one is going to knock on your door or call

† LinkedIn—a social media platform for managing your professional identity.

your cell and say, "I want to hire you." Empower yourself, be proactive, and create opportunities for yourself.

RÉSUMÉ AND COVER LETTER

Creating a resume for yourself and thinking that you don't have work experience is common—so what can you possibly put on there? Don't sell yourself short. Think about the volunteer opportunities you had in high school. Think about the babysitting job you held for three years, or the lawns that you mowed for free for your neighbors. What about the clubs or organizations that you were part of in high school? If you were part of school government, math club, or even on a sports team, then use it. Yes, it all counts as experience. Using specific keywords on your résumé is advantageous for your search. Instead of writing "showed leadership skills," write "demonstrated leadership skills." Instead of writing "supported math department," write "advised math department." These small changes create a huge impact on your résumé.

You can find basic templates at youre18nowwhat.com, or just use this QR code.

NETWORKING

First, never underestimate the power of networking. Second, use your network to your advantage. So, the question is, how do you network? You might not realize that networking begins when you start making friends and creating relationships. When we create an environment for ourselves that surrounds us with people we like, people we respect and who respect us, and people who will bring us up when we are feeling down, we are building a solid network.

Generally, people like to work with people who they feel comfortable with, who they like, and who they respect. Much of finding a job or internship is still who you know, not what you know. Meaning that it takes who you know to get you in the door, and what you know to keep you in the room. By utilizing your connections, you can get a sense of what people in your network are doing for work, and what interests you—don't be afraid to ask people what they like or dislike about their job. Ask about their role at their company—how they started, how is it going, if there is space for growth and opportunity, and what kind of benefits are offered.

> What will you do for networking?

INTERVIEW DRESS, PREPARATION, AND QUESTIONS

The interview process can be a little nerve-wracking, but with practice, you will be successful. The first step is dressing for the part. What industry are you applying for? Why does this matter? If you are applying for a creative position in marketing or media, then the dress code is less formal—typically, dress pants and a shirt will do for any gender.

If you are applying for a position in banking or finance, then it is more formal and you should wear a suit, whether that is a pantsuit or a skirt suit or a dress with a jacket, but it should be a suit. Myself, I currently work in academia and can wear conservative or casual clothes. I go back and forth and wear both, but I will never forget the time I was told to dress for the job I wanted, not the job I had. So, if I am the most conservatively dressed most days, I don't mind at all. I happen to love wearing suits, or dresses with boots to be more comfortable.

Your dress code for the interview also shows your personality. Your clothes reflect not only how you look but how you feel. If you dress confidently, you feel confident, and that confidence will come through in the interview process.

It's the same when you go out with friends—how you dress determines how you feel. If you wear sweats and a tee to go out, then you are telling yourself and others that you just want to hang out and relax. If you wear nice jeans or pants with a great shirt and shoes then you are saying "I feel good, I look good, and I want that to be represented."

Dress to impress.

So now that you have an interview, what's next? Preparation is a key component of any interview. You should look up the company and read about the culture, initiatives, and strategic plan. Here are some questions to ask yourself as you do your preparation:

1. What experiences do you have that resonate with the company you are applying to?
2. What are you bringing to the role that you are applying to?
3. Do your personal culture and values resonate with the company?
4. Have you spoken to anyone at the company who has given positive feedback where you feel comfortable being yourself?

Many people are nervous in an interview setting, and that is totally understandable. What I think people don't realize is that the interview is your opportunity to ask questions. You should be able to interview them just as much as they are interviewing you. It should be conversational—not interrogative.

Don't be afraid to ask:

1. How long has the position been open?
2. Why did the last two or three people leave the company?
3. Is there an opportunity for growth?
4. When are you looking to fill the position?
5. What are the expectations of the role for the first ninety days?

If you have not looked up the benefits, now is the perfect time to ask about them. Benefits can be separated into three different buckets:[‡]

1. What is required by law?
2. What is the industry standard?
3. What are fringe benefits?

WHAT IS REQUIRED BY LAW?

Mandatory benefits include worker's compensation insurance (which provides cash benefits or medical care to employees who become injured or ill on the job), unemployment insurance (a federal and state program that provides monetary benefits to eligible employees who are laid-off and seeking new employment), and, in some state and local laws, paid sick leave (paid time off from work to address your health needs, which is different from PTO time).

‡ SHRM.org, 2023

WHAT IS THE INDUSTRY STANDARD?

An industry standard benefit package is one that includes some degree of health care coverage (this can be medical, dental, and/or vision). Some companies offer this at no cost if the only insured person will be the employee—there is usually a cost to add a spouse, partner, or children to the health plan, which is covered in more detail in Chapter 6. A savings or 401(k) plan is an industry standard, but some small companies do not offer a match to the savings plan as some large companies do (we will dive deeper into the 401(k) in Chapter 9). A few fringe benefits in some industries are considered standard, such as fast-growing high-tech companies that offer contributions toward health club memberships or meal reimbursement if you work through dinner.

WHAT ARE FRINGE BENEFITS?

Fringe benefits are anything extra that you can imagine a job offering you. These are known as noncash compensation programs that show employee appreciation and help with motivation and productivity among employees. These benefits can include paid time off (PTO is a pool of bankable hours that can be used for any purpose), corporate or gym memberships, meals, a company car, tuition reimbursement (recall this from Chapter 2), childcare assistance, and employee discounts on products and services.

NEGOTIATING SALARY AND ASKING FOR A RAISE!

Negotiating your salary and asking for what you are worth for a particular job is not easy for everyone. Again, there are resources available to you where you can find the industry standard for what a position pays. Glassdoor[§] is a great resource where you can browse open jobs but also check company reviews—what do past and current employees say about the company, the culture, the pay, the management? All the information is there for review. What is the current salary of a chef in Phoenix, Arizona? By signing up for a free account, you can enter your information, education, experience, and location to see what the job market is paying.

Another piece of information I like to pass on is to turn the question of salary onto the person interviewing you. It is a tricky situation because they are asking you how much money you want to make. You don't want to aim too low and seem desperate, and you don't want to aim too high that they dismiss what you're asking.

What I say in interviews is that I know what I bring to the role with my experience and education, and I don't want to discount myself from the position, but what is the budget for the role? Every position has a budget—a low and a high—and hopefully the recruiter has already discussed that with you. This gives you the opportunity to say, "I know that the range for the role which I am applying is $x to $y and I feel that with my current expertise I should be at the higher end of the salary."

Then you say nothing. Let that sink in for the interviewer and just wait. They will either agree or disagree with you. If they agree, that is great. If they do not agree, all is not lost. Here is where you can negotiate other benefits or say, "Thank you. Is there an opportunity for reevaluation after three months into the role?" Remember to follow up on this three-month or six-month evaluation. During your first few months in the new role, keep track of what you have been doing, what extra tasks you have taken on; in other words, create a brag sheet for yourself for

§ Glassdoor.com—a free resource to search jobs and company reviews.

Remember that an interview goes both ways.

when the evaluation conversation takes place. You will be glad you did, and remember that it is business, not personal.

FORMS

Congratulations on securing your first job! The most overwhelming part might be filling out all the new hire paperwork and not knowing what the forms are for since you have not done this before. It is not the same as getting hired as a babysitter or cutting lawns on the weekends while in high school. These are forms that are required by law that will also tie into when you begin to file taxes, which is covered in Chapter 8. This is all tracked for as long as you work and will be used for how much social security you will receive upon retirement, which will be covered in Chapter 9. So, what forms should you be aware of?

W-4 form (Federal Income Tax Withholding): filled out by the employee when they accept a new job or at any time after if the employee wants to change their filing status (ex. "single" changed to "married" or "married" changed to add dependents).

W-2 Form: filled out by the employer at the end of each year. It is a statement of employee earnings and tax withholdings for that tax year (which is needed to file taxes).

I-9 Employment Eligibility Form: used to verify the identity and employment authorization of individuals hired for employment in the United States (uscis.gov, 2023). The employee must provide documentation (passport, permanent resident card, etc. or driver's license and social security card or birth certificate—details of acceptable forms of ID are on the form).

State Tax Withholding Form: vary by state and the employer will provide them.

In addition, there will be other new hire forms to complete and many of them will be provided electronically and may include demographic and administrative forms, direct deposit forms, employee contract, and health and benefit forms. Some companies will issue a welcome letter, an employee handbook, and perhaps a computer and other equipment so you can be successful. If you work for a large company, you might even receive some company swag, so enjoy!

Chapter 5

I CAN . . . UNDERSTAND HEALTH INSURANCE

It's a great feeling when you secure that first job. Now that the stress and anxiety of all the interviews that you went through are over, it is time to focus on what the company is offering. You negotiated a salary with a benefit package, so how do you navigate the different benefits and signing up for the ones that you need or want?

Most companies will offer a benefits training session, whether in person, virtual, or with a mentor, and I highly recommend attending. It is one thing to read through the benefit package and another to understand it—so ask questions.

MEDICAL, DENTAL, AND VISION

Medical insurance is the legal entitlement to payment or reimbursement for your health care costs. This is either through a contract with a health insurance company (typically business owners), a group health plan offered with employment, or a government program like Medicare (providing care for those over sixty-five, or younger individuals with disabilities), Medicaid (providing aid for those with limited income and resources), or the Children's Health Insurance Program (CHIP).

Here we are discussing health plans offered through your employer. There are different health care companies (Aetna, Blue Cross Blue Shield, Cigna, Humana, United Health Care, to name a few) and what is offered will depend upon the organization. The state where you work will affect the coverage as well. Some employers will give free health insurance coverage if you are the only one being insured. If you need to add a spouse, partner, or children to be covered as well, then the cost of coverage will increase.

The most common medical coverage is offered as a choice between a Health Maintenance Organization (HMO) plan and a Preferred Provider Organization (PPO) plan. With an HMO, the premiums are lower, and you have less out-of-pocket costs. Individuals choose a primary care physician from a network of providers. If you need to see a specialist, you must go to your primary care physician first and then get a referral to see the specialist. Network restrictions help control costs by directing individuals to network providers who have negotiated rates with the HMO.

The pros of an HMO are cost savings, preventative care emphasis, and coordinated care. The cons are the limited choice of providers, the need for referrals, and limited or no out-of-network coverage.

PPOs are more flexible for selecting healthcare providers, allowing individuals to go out of network without referrals, but with higher premiums and costs. Although a PPO has a slightly higher monthly premium and out-of-pocket expenses, you also have access to a much larger network of providers. Even if you go out of network, some costs are covered, but you will have a separate deductible to meet.

The pros of a PPO are flexibility and greater provider choice, out-of-network coverage, and direct specialist access without needing a referral. The cons are the higher cost, out-of-network expenses (if incurred), and network limitations to receive the maximum benefits and most comprehensive coverage.

Is an HMO or a PPO
a better choice for you right now?

When choosing a plan for yourself, think about your current primary care physician and if they fall into your network. Think about any specialists that you see on a regular basis. What are your personal health needs and preferences? What are your budget and financial considerations? What about accessibility and convenience—where are the locations of the providers that you are choosing? Answers to these questions can help with your decision, but know that both plans promote regular check-ups and preventative care.

Dental plans work in a similar way to medical coverage with both in-network and out-of-network coverage. Most dental plans offer preventative and diagnostic care (check-ups, cleanings, X-rays) covering the full cost of these services, or with a small copay. For basic restorative services (fillings, root canals), most of the costs will be covered, and it is common to have a waiting period for these services and deductibles that must be met before payment from the plan.

Major restorative services (crowns, bridges, implants) are only covered for about half of the costs and there can be waiting periods for these treatments. Many dental plans are managed plans that require you to choose a dentist from a pre-approved list where the providers have agreed to discount their fees. In general, dental HMOs will not provide any coverage if the member receives care from a provider who is not in network.

Again, choosing a dental plan is dependent upon your current dental health needs, costs that can be involved, and the coverage will depend on the state where you work as well. According to the Journal of the American Dental Association (2022), the cost of dental care is more of a barrier to consumers than it is for medical care, prescriptions, mental health care, or vision care.

Vision coverage can be in the form of a vision plan or vision insurance. These plans help protect your eye health and ensure you have access to eyeglasses or contacts. Some vision plans offer an eye exam once per year and discounts on eyeglass frames and lenses once every year or two depending on the plan. See your company plan for the specifics of your insurance.

There are some plans that will offer a discount for Lasik surgery as most companies will not cover it since it is considered an elective procedure. Vision insurance will offer either a vision benefits package or discounts on eye care. They might require paying a deductible and a copay at each visit. With a vision discount plan, you will pay for services but receive a discount on the fees.

Other insurance might include a Flexible Spending Account (FSA—sometimes referred to as flexible spending arrangement) or Health Savings Account (HSA), which is an account you put money into that can be used to pay for certain out-of-pocket health care costs. You do not pay taxes on this money, meaning you will save an amount equal to the taxes you would have paid on the money you put aside.

These types of accounts are good to have depending on the extent of your health care or dependent care costs. It is important to note that if you contribute more than you spend, any unused funds may disappear if your employer does not roll them over. Check this toward the end of the year to be sure you are not losing money.

> **If you have access to an FSA or an HSA, take advantage of them.**

A health care FSA can be used for medical expenses, over-the-counter items (allergy, sinus, digestive care medications, or first-aid items, to name a few), medical equipment (insulin, bandages, cold and flu medicine, reading glasses, etc.), dental, and vision care.

A dependent care FSA can cover costs like preschool, summer day camp, and day care for children, adult children under the age of twenty-six, or a dependent adult. Depending on the benefit plan, your employer may contribute to the FSA too. You may have to submit receipts and documentation for reimbursement of items, or you may have a debit card associated with the FSA account that you can use.

An HSA account works the same way as an FSA as both can help save for qualified medical expenses. HSAs differ in that they are employee owned, may offer higher contributions by the employee, and allow you to carry the funds over if you are enrolled in an HSA-eligible health plan. As of 2021, the contribution limit for an FSA account was $2,750, and for an HSA account, it was $3,600 for an individual or $7,200 for a family.

COPAYS, COINSURANCE, AND DEDUCTIBLES

Copays, coinsurance, and deductibles come up often when speaking about medical, dental, vision, and other health insurance coverage. Whether you have an HMO or PPO health care plan, these are the basics:

PREMIUM	DEDUCTIBLE	COPAY
The amount of money you pay each month for insurance	The amount you pay for health expenses before your insurance company begins to cover most costs	A smaller, fixed out-of-pocket cost you cover for healthcare, usually after you meet your deductible
COINSURANCE	**ALLOWED AMOUNT**	**OUT-OF-POCKET MAXIMUM**
Percentage of the cost you cover for a service after you've reached your deductible	Maximum cost your insurance will pay for a service	Maximum cost you have to cover before your insurance begins covering 100% of covered costs

SHORT- AND LONG-TERM DISABILITY AND FMLA

When we speak about benefits that a company offers, short- and long-term disability and FMLA are top of conversation. When you need some time off from work for an extended period, it weighs heavily on both the employer and the employee. Short-term disability is a type of insurance that will partially cover your income (about 50–70 percent) while you are away and cannot perform your job duties due to an illness or an injury. This illness or injury is usually temporary—someone giving birth and needing time off, or someone breaking their wrist or hand so they cannot work for a bit of time.

Some companies offer short-term disability, and some do not. If your company does not offer short-term disability coverage, you can purchase it from a private insurance company.

Where short-term disability covers a portion of your income, the Family and Medical Leave Act* (FMLA), which is a law, protects your job. FMLA leave can provide up to twelve weeks of time off for an illness, injury, or to care for a family member. There are some stipulations with FMLA, and you can use it if you:

1. Work for a public agency or company with at least fifty employees.
2. Have worked for at least twelve months.
3. Have logged at least 1,250 hours of work during the twelve months before taking leave.
4. Work in a location which has at least fifty employees within seventy-five miles.

With short-term disability, it is typical to just have worked ninety days to be eligible, and some companies extend beyond the twelve weeks up to twenty-six weeks or more. Short term disability is for the employee only and has a certain waiting period, which can differ from employer to employer (some require vacation or sick leave to be used first).

When thinking about taking leave, it is a great idea to sit down with the person in the benefits department and ask all the questions needed to make the best-informed decision.

1. What is the time off needed (for myself or someone else)?

---

* FMLA does not require the employer to pay the employee taking a leave of absence.

2. Can I afford to sacrifice receiving an income?
3. Is twelve weeks enough time off?
4. What kind of documentation can I provide for the time off that is needed?
5. What are the disability benefits and are they taxable?

Long-term disability works in tandem with short-term disability, and when the short-term benefits are exhausted, long-term benefits will begin. You will need to provide medical proof (of chronic illness, cancer treatments, or other debilitating illness or injury that lasts longer than twenty-six weeks) that you need longer time away from work and will need medical clearance to return to work. Benefits will continue until you are cleared, or your benefits have been exhausted. Long-term disability will pay benefits of about 60–80 percent of your income for a longer period than twelve weeks, and typically two, five, or even ten years, or for the life of the policyholder. The average cost for both short- or long-term disability is about 1–3 percent of your pre-tax wages. Some companies offer long-term disability, while others require you to opt-in and pay for the long-term disability coverage. You can also obtain benefits through a private insurance company.

STRESS AND HEALTH

Other insurance benefits that people are not familiar with are the ones that concern our stress and wellness on a regular basis. Most insurance companies have a webpage that few employees visit, but there is an abundance of information available from free webinars on wellness, smoking cessation programs, gym membership discounts, chiropractors, therapists, and where to find free flu shots.

There are health challenges that can be completed to receive further discounts and sometimes gift cards from retailers. You can only know what your company is offering in benefits if you actually read the information and see how it can help you and your health. Again, this is something that you need to take ownership of because your parents may call and check on you to see if you went to that eye doctor, or that dentist you mentioned on a call last week. Amazing how they don't forget those things!

Chapter 6

I CAN . . . BUY OR LEASE A CAR

Cars! Wow, do I love cars! I think it is what got me into the finance space. I have an uncle who I love dearly, and I remember when he came to visit us in Brooklyn, he always had an amazing car. One year he showed up with a 1968 Corvette Stingray in a not quite kelly green color and I instantly fell in love. It was a used one, but it was my uncle's. I remember asking my mom what he did for work because I wanted to do what he did so I could buy a nice car when I grew up. It didn't help that I had three brothers who loved cars as well. They would teach me about the styles and designs and engines—it was great. I was hooked.

Finally getting my wheels!

What I learned is that it would take a long time to get that fancy car. It didn't happen overnight, as nothing ever does. I was willing to work—and I was willing to wait. I lived in a city and there was plenty of public transportation, so I knew I had time. I wanted a car, any car; then I wanted a new car; then I wanted a nice car; and finally, I wanted the fancy car. Over the years I have leased my cars because I wanted a new one every few years. I also don't love any one car so much that I want to keep it for eight or ten years. Let's see what it entails to get a car and what the best options are for you.

Getting your first car is one of the most exciting milestones in a person's life. You have probably been thinking about a car since you started studying for the permit test, knowing that you will have a license soon.

What freedom to be able to drive yourself where you want, and when you want! It takes some time, but you will get there. So, what is the next step? Do you have some money saved? Will your parents or guardians help with your first purchase? What is your budget? Are you looking to buy a new or used car? Maybe lease a car, instead?

BUYING A CAR

Well, let's talk about your credit score again. Remember Chapter 1? Just like you need a good credit score to get an apartment, or a job, you need a good score to get a car as well. Unless, of course, you are just going to write a check and pay it in full. Not many people can do that, but if you are buying a used car, that is a possibility.

Buying a car is similar to buying a house because you will own it and build equity. Unlike a house, which appreciates over time, a car is probably the biggest depreciating asset you can own. When you buy a car, the minute you drive it off the lot, you lose about 10–15 percent of the value of the vehicle (depending on the make and model). Why? It's because now the vehicle is used and not new.

When you buy a car, you will have financing options where you can take out a loan for typically thirty-six to eighty-four months. The average car loan "is 68.6 and 67.4 months for new and used cars, respectively, and 35.3 months for leased vehicles" (Lending Tree, 2023).[†] You can choose to find a loan on your own (through Lending Tree, Capital One, etc.) or use one of the lenders that the dealership uses. The dealership where you purchase your car will have relationships with different banks to get their customers the best rates.

Knowing your credit score before you get to the dealership should give you an indication of where your loan rate will fall. Remember, the better the score, the lower the term, the better the rate. Car dealerships also have special deals that are run each month and maybe offer a 2.99 percent APR for a car loan on a new car. Look into the different deals at the dealership you anticipate going to so you have a sense of what you will be paying.

If you have a monthly budget in mind, let the dealership know you want to stay under that. It is about sales for the dealership and about getting the best deal for yourself. If your budget is $400 a month for a car, tell the dealership your budget is $350. Once you add in extras like wheel and tire coverage, extended warranties, or something else, you will be closer to your $400 target and will still feel comfortable with the payment. Sometimes it is worth extending the loan to get the payment you want, so if you have a thirty-six-month loan at $500 a month, you can change that to a forty-eight-month loan at $375 or $400 (depending on if the rate is the same or not—so be sure to ask about that too).[‡]

There is also no prepayment penalty if you want to add extra money to the principal of the loan each month. This will shorten the

† Lending Tree—one of the nation's largest online networks for funding loans
‡ The dollar amounts represented here are fictitious.

Purchase or lease?

life of the loan, and, at the end of your payments, you will own an asset. You can continue to keep that car and complete maintenance on it to keep it running smoothly. You can also continue to make payments on it—this time to yourself to increase your savings. You already have the amount allocated each month in your budget—why not add all or part of it to your nest egg?

LEASING A CAR

Leasing a car is what I love to do because it gives me the option of having a new car and being able to get another new car every few years. The downside is that leasing a car is like renting an apartment—while I lease my car, I am renting it, meaning I do not have any ownership of it at all. The upside to leasing a car is that the payments are lower for leasing a car than buying a car. It allows a person to get a higher-priced automobile for the same price as buying a less expensive automobile. So, if you have a budget of $400 per month (as used in the example above), you can purchase a car that sells for about $18,000–$20,000; but if you spend that same $400 on a leased vehicle, the worth of that car will be about $30,000–$35,000.[§]

Leasing allows a person to drive a higher-priced vehicle and have the lease for twenty-four to thirty-nine months. Most leases are thirty-six months in duration. There are dealership incentives that are given with leases, just as there are with purchases. Sometimes getting 10,000 miles per year on a lease is more expensive than getting 12,000

§ The dollar amounts represented here are fictitious.

miles a year. Sometimes a thirty-six-month payment is less expensive than a thirty-nine-month payment because the incentive is on selling the thirty-six-month payment.

Another plus to leasing a vehicle is that you are driving it during the time the manufacturer's warranty is in effect, so no worries about faulty computer systems—they are typically covered. Your leased vehicle will have the latest safety features and you don't need to worry about trade-in values or selling it when the lease it up. If you don't drive more than 10,000–12,000 miles per year, this might be an option for you.

Ask these questions about a lease:

1. How long is the term of the lease?
2. How many miles per year do I get with the lease? (More expensive cars give fewer annual miles.)
3. What is the cost per mile if I go over the lease amount? (These can range from $0.15 to $0.50 per mile over—which can become costly.)
4. Is there maintenance coverage that comes with the lease? (Some dealerships offer the first oil change free; some offer two years of basic maintenance.)

Even at the end of the lease, you have options. You can bring the car back to the dealer where you leased it from, just return it, walk away (literally, because you will not have a car), and be done. Or you can purchase the car at the end of the lease.

If you decide that you love the car, you can purchase it by either calling the finance company that the lease is with or going back to the dealership to complete the process. Please note that you will need to qualify for financing as if you were never there before. The good news is that you had financing before and hopefully paid the payments on time and increased your credit score in the process, so they know you are creditworthy. It should be a smooth transition to do this.

The third option for the lease end is to bring the car to any dealer of any automobile that you want and turn in the old lease for a new one. This is my preferred option and allows me to switch between different automobiles so I can lease a Nissan, a Mercedes, a Lexus, a Cadillac, or whatever I choose. When you have a thirty-six- or thirty-nine-month lease (which is standard) you can usually trade in your lease for a new one about three or four months before the lease ends.

This allows you to not worry about the mileage (unless you have gone significantly over) on your Mercedes because the Cadillac dealer is going to take that car and sell it. It allows you to have flexibility in leasing something new, and if you plan on leasing an electric vehicle (EV), you could qualify for a $7,500 tax credit.[¶] You are covered on a lease for basic wear and tear of the vehicle and are responsible for basic maintenance. You typically cannot alter the vehicle, as that would void any warranty that you have on it—remember, you do not own it.

There are upfront costs whether you buy or lease a vehicle. For purchases, these are any down payments, taxes, registration, or other fees. For a lease, it may include the first month's payment, an acquisition fee, taxes, registration, or other fees. Very rarely do I put down money on a lease. Usually if they are asking for $2,000 down, I will have them put that money into the payments. For leases, it averages about $27 per $1,000, meaning a $2,000 down payment would increase my monthly payment by $54 ($27 x 2) bringing it to $454 per month instead of $400 (the amount used in previous examples).

¶ Consumer Reports is a nonprofit consumer organization dedicated to independent product testing, investigative journalism, consumer-oriented research, public education, and consumer advocacy.

Whether you buy or lease a car, be sure to find a reputable dealership, do some research on the car, some research on the rates, and by all means ask questions.

INSURANCE AND DEDUCTIBLES

Insurance—again? Well, yes. Now we need to cover insurance for your recently purchased or leased vehicle. Recall that insurance is something that we purchase to hedge against a risk of loss or harm. With car insurance, the US laws help protect individuals involved in accidents that are not their fault. For some states, you need to prove that you have car insurance before you leave the lot with your car; other states require that you have coverage within seven days.

It is a fairly simple process. Call the company you want to have insurance with and let them know you just purchased or leased a car. You will give them the vehicle identification number (VIN), and they will let you know the cost. Similar to renter's or homeowner's insurance, you can pay for it either monthly or every six months.

There is collision insurance and comprehensive insurance. Not all states require this coverage, and if you purchased an older car, it might not be worth it to have this coverage. Collision coverage helps to pay for damage done to your car in the case of an accident, regardless of who is at fault. Comprehensive coverage helps to pay for damages done to your car in non-collision accidents. This can include damage from natural disasters, vandalism, or theft. Car insurance is important to have if you decide to lend your car to a friend or relative. Your coverage follows the car, so it would cover most of the claims if your friend or relative were driving.

There are factors that go into the cost of car insurance including the age of the car (an older car can cost less than a newer car), the make and model of the car (luxury vehicles cost more because the market value is higher and the cost to repair is higher), and the risk of theft (some cars are more frequently broken into than others). A car accident can be costly even if you are not at fault.

In general, it is a good idea to shop around for different quotes and see the different coverage amounts for your vehicle. Ask questions to find the right coverage, which can vary from $10,000 per person or $20,000 per accident for bodily coverage to a maximum of $300,000 or $500,000 per accident for liability coverage. The deductible is important because that is the amount that you will need to pay out of pocket before the insurance company steps in and pays. If you have a $500 deductible and the damage to your car is $1,500, then you will pay the $500 and the insurance company will pay the $1,000. If you have a deductible that is $1,000 and the damage is $1,500, then you will pay the $1,000 and the insurance company will pay the $500. The premiums are typically higher if you have a low deductible, and lower if you have a higher deductible. A common policy structure is 250/500/100, and this is a simplified version of what that means:

250	500	100
Bodily injury coverage, meaning $250,000 for injuries per person	Overall maximum coverage, meaning $500,000 for injuries total per accident	Property damage coverage, meaning $100,000 for property damage per accident

RENTAL COVERAGE

There are companies that offer rental car coverage through your car insurance policy, and this is typically a low cost per month. Just in case you have an incident, your insurance company will cover up to a certain amount per day for a rental car. That amount varies with the type of coverage you have, so check the details of your policy. The question is, are the few dollars per month worth it if you need to rent a car for three days, a week, or a month? If you have a multiple car household, you might not need the extra coverage.

Chapter 7

I CAN . . . TRAVEL

Travel can be an amazing part of life, whether you plan to travel regionally, nationally, or globally. There are so many places to see and many things to do. What interests you—relaxing at a beach or resort, hiking and climbing trails, taking a cruise to a specific destination? As rewarding of an experience as traveling is, it takes planning and some research.

CULTURE

Once you decide on where you are going, it is time to dive into some research. If you are traveling within your own country, you want to look at the local places that people frequent. There are some tourist spots everywhere, but looking outside of those and seeing what the locals do helps to connect you to the people in the area and really get an insight into what the everyday might look like. Check out Instagram posts or ask friends who have been to the area before. Many

> **Respect and embrace other cultures**
>
> **—step outside your comfort zone.**

people are willing to share what they loved about a destination; they are also willing to share what was not so great or disappointing. Of course, this information is subjective, but if there are many people saying either good or bad things, it can be justified to believe the talk.

When you are planning your visit, ask questions such as:

1. What are the best trails to walk or bike?
2. Do they have museums or art galleries that host local artists?
3. Is there a particular music festival that the area is known for?
4. Where do the locals eat?

Some people like to think when they are away—especially if they go back and visit a familiar place multiple years in a row—what would it be like if I moved there? You can only get that feel if you visit at least a few times and do what the locals do.

What do you know about the area? What do you know about the culture? These are crucial questions especially if traveling internationally. Understanding the culture of the place you are visiting and even sometimes understanding the language—even if it is just a few key words—helps to connect you to the people and they will see the respect you have for their community. Sometimes knowing basic phrases can go a long way when asking for directions to the local coffee shop. Just a simple "please" or "thank you" in their language is a pleasantry.

> **Who knew there are laws and regulations different from what I am accustomed to?**

Are there any laws, customs, or safety concerns that you need to be aware of? Think about any political or socio-economic issues within countries. As with any large city, be careful of your surroundings when traveling or walking around. I have heard stories where you can be in the middle of the sidewalk just looking at your phone for something, and someone will come by on a bicycle and snap it up in a second.

It can help to share your itinerary with someone you trust so they know your whereabouts. It is wise not to flaunt expensive jewelry or electronics—or to count cash out in the open. And always walk along well-lit areas at night.

Is it a conservative area? You may not realize, but this can be important for dress code—you do not want to be offensive by inappropriate attire. Your attire can help you blend in with the local community.

What are the norms for a greeting or tipping at hotels and restaurants? For greetings, is it a handshake, a hug, a bow, or a smile? Be observant of these small gestures. For tipping, it varies from place to place. Check the bill—it is possible that it might be added already, and you don't want to over-tip or under-tip.

Tipping in the United States is not the same as tipping in Europe. When you can, tip in cash and use local currency (having some small bills in local currency can be helpful). In general, for restaurants, the norm for some countries is between 10 and 20 percent, where in others, it is less than that or not expected at all. It can even be considered rude to tip. The more you know, the more enjoyable the experience will be.

TRANSPORTATION

Flights, trains, public transportation—it can be overwhelming. Planning is crucial to know how to get around. In some places, flights are less expensive than trains, and public transportation can be more time-consuming than taking a taxi. However you decide to travel, make sure that you have your documents in order: a driver's license or state identification card. If you need a passport for where you are traveling, be sure to make a few copies of your documents—keep one copy at home and keep the other copy with you—separate from the originals, just in case the documents get lost or stolen.

Are there any visas or permits required? There are customs declarations that need to be completed upon arrival to your destination country. If you are traveling to more than one country, you will likely need to complete the customs declaration form for each one.

Do you need any vaccines to travel to the area you are headed to? Certain countries require vaccinations to be current (some even require that the vaccine is not less than six months to expiry). Be sure to carry any vaccination cards or medications needed and have a small first-aid kit on hand just in case.

Payments for travel? Really?

This is where you can utilize your credit card to work for you. What card do you have that gives you back rewards? What type of rewards program does the card offer? Some credit cards offer cash back on purchases or miles that can be used on transportation or hotels. Before you set out to travel, think about what cards will be most beneficial for your needs. You can look into Wallethub.com to see what the experts have to say about different cards for different purposes and the pros and cons of each. Sites like this and others fact-check the information they receive from the experts in the field that they speak with.

When traveling, it is a good idea to carry a mix of payments including cash, a credit card, and a backup credit card. Keep some local currency on hand as well. Be careful not to use your debit card while traveling. When you do this, the merchant can put an extended hold on funds in your checking account for booking a hotel or renting a car. If there is an issue with the card, it will take a while to get the funds back into your account.

What about insurance for when you travel? Travel insurance is financial protection in case of cancellations, medical emergencies, or any unforeseen circumstance that would prevent you from traveling. Travel insurance can include anything from emergency medical coverage, if you become ill or injured while traveling, to covering your baggage or personal belongings, just in case of loss, damage, or stolen items.

> This insurance thing keeps coming up.

When renting a car, the rental company might offer insurance for you, but it is wise to check your personal car insurance policy before you travel. Many times, your personal coverage will extend to covering you when you rent a car, so there is no need to add any additional costs to your rental. There are also credit cards that you can use that might offer insurance coverage by using that card, so check with your credit card company.

BOOKING A PLACE TO STAY

There is an abundance of options when booking a place to stay during travel. From hotels to vacation rentals to hostels or an Airbnb.

First and foremost, book something that is within your budget. Just because you are on vacation does not mean foregoing the budget. Find a well-reviewed, reputable accommodation. The most expensive place is not necessarily the best place to stay, just as the least expensive is not going to be the worst place to stay. Look at the reviews and listen to friends and family if they have been there and be sure to book well in advance—especially during what might be considered "peak season" for the area.

When out and about, carry only the essential items you need and use the hotel safe for an added level of security if you need. If you are in a vacation rental or Airbnb, check the requirements for staying there. Unlike at a hotel, you might be required to empty the garbage or run the dishwasher and strip the beds before you check out. There might also be additional fees for cleaning services. Take this into consideration when you make accommodations—how much or how little do you want to be responsible for in the room or house?

MISCELLANEOUS

Another basic thing to think about when traveling is packing, so check the weather and compare that to the activities you have planned. Take your chargers and any adapters for your electronics and have them fully charged before you head out for the day (it is not always easy to get back to your room in the middle of the day if your device should lose power). Investing in a water bottle with a built-in filter is a plus, especially if traveling where the drinking water is not safe. It is also a cost savings if you can bring your water with you each day.

Traveling is an experience, and although it might have some challenges, embrace the change, the food, the connections, and the memories. It can be as adventurous, exciting, or as relaxing as you like, and you can make lifelong friendships along the way. It can be part of your personal growth and getting out of your comfort zone. Simply taking a break from your routine can have positive effects on your mental and physical health, so take the time and explore, knowing that you'll be back again to enjoy another journey.

Chapter 8

I CAN . . . UNDERSTAND TAXES AND HOW THEY AFFECT ME

The job has been going well and you are learning so many things that you are probably surprised you can keep up with it all. Just a short while ago, you finished your studies and secured a great job. When you began the job, I am sure the nerves started, which is true at any stage of life with any new job, but a few weeks in and the confidence is kicking in.

Woohoo—getting my first real check!

You are also amazed at how much you are remembering what you learned in specific courses and how they relate to the real-world experience you are getting now. As you go forward in your career, these experiences will continue to build upon the education you received, and the more confident you will become in your abilities. Have strength in that, but let's get into how to understand all those numbers on your paycheck!

UNDERSTANDING MY PAYCHECK

The days of actually receiving a paper check are long gone. Most companies will direct deposit your paycheck into an account that you choose. You can choose to deposit the entire paycheck into your checking account, or some companies have an option to have the money split. You can deposit 90 percent into your checking account and 10 percent into your savings account (or you can choose any combination that totals 100 percent).

I find that this is a good way to save extra money each pay period because when it is automatically sent to a savings account, and you get accustomed to having a certain amount in your checking (which is usually your spending account), you are less likely to touch the savings account.

Wow—that's a lot of information on that check.

There are a few companies that process checks and the most widely used is Automated Data Processing, Inc. (ADP). ADP has an app that can be downloaded on your phone, and you can review your pay to see if it is correct. Aside from the basic personal information that is on your paycheck (name, address, employee ID), there is your employer's name and address listed. It will have the pay period listed on it, showing a weekly, biweekly, or monthly pay period. Your paystub will also show your gross earnings, net earnings, taxes, and deductions.

Gross earnings are the total amount before any deductions and include hourly wage or salary, overtime, bonuses, or commissions paid. Your net earnings—the amount that is deposited into your account, known as take-home pay—is the amount after all the deductions have been taken out. These deductions are any health insurance premiums, life insurance, disability benefits, or an FSA or HSA account that you signed up for (recall Chapter 5). You will also see deductions for taxes:

Federal Income Tax: this tax is determined by your income level and the W-4 form you filled out upon hiring.

State Income Tax: this tax is collected in most states to cover state costs (usually funding for education, building and repairing bridges and tunnels, or health care coverage for low-income families and their children).

Local Income Tax: this tax is collected in some areas to cover local costs (usually police and fire services, libraries, road maintenance, and other programs and projects that will benefit the local community).

Social Security Tax and Medicare Tax: these are mandatory payroll taxes that fund the Social Security and Medicare programs. These deductions are usually a fixed percentage of your gross earnings.

Pre-Tax and Post-Tax Deductions: pre-tax deductions are taken before regular taxes and can lower your tax bracket, ultimately reducing your tax liability when you file your taxes at the end of the year. These can be for health insurance, commuter benefits, or for retirement contributions, which will be covered in Chapter 9. Post-tax deductions are taken after taxes and can include disability insurance or a Roth IRA contribution, which is also covered in Chapter 9.

Your paycheck will show your current pay period earnings and your year-to-date (YTD) earnings. It is imperative to check your information, especially when starting a new job, to be certain that your information is correct, your deductions (both pre-tax and post-tax) are correct, and that your agreed-upon salary is correct. If there are questions or if you notice any discrepancies, you should reach out to your human resources or payroll department (some companies have two separate departments, and some have only one).

FILING TAXES

Filing taxes is mandatory for each person who receives a paycheck. It is the process of reporting your income, expenses, and any other financial information to the government to determine if you have paid enough taxes throughout the year, or if you are entitled to a refund if you paid too much in taxes. For most people starting out in their career, you can file a 1040 form, which is straightforward and is for taxpayers with basic tax situations and quick and easy filing. It is a simple form to fill out and does not include room for itemized deductions and complex investment income. It is a two-page form available to file online (irs.gov., 2023).

> Filing taxes is not as scary as it seems—you can do this!

There are different people who can assist with taxes. Tax preparers, tax specialists, and tax associates are interchangeable titles for people who can assist with basic tax preparations. They must show competence (a license) from a formal exam, or Internal Revenue Service (IRS) employment. To be a paid tax return preparer, you must have an IRS Preparer Tax Identification Number (PTIN). A Certified Public Accountant, or CPA, is a licensed professional with advanced education and training in areas of accounting and business.

Tax analysts can work for individuals or corporations handling tax audits and tax compliance and have skills in financial analysis, payroll, and external auditing. They are responsible for making individuals and businesses aware of ways to reduce their tax liability and payments.

If you want to check a person's credentials, you can look them up on the Return Preparer Office (RPO) directory to research tax return preparers in your area. Only persons "with a PTIN who hold a professional credential or have obtained an Annual Filing Season Program Record of Completion from the IRS" are listed in the directory, which is updated regularly, although it can take up to four weeks for a "preparer's information to be added or revised".*

The biggest question people have asked is, "Do I claim 0 or 1 for myself on the W-4 form?" When you fill out your W-4 form, you are choosing the amount of taxes to be taken on your behalf, and that is decided by the total number allowance you claim. By placing a "0" on line 5, you are indicating that you want the most amount of tax taken out of your pay each pay period. If you claim "1" for yourself instead, then less is taken out of your pay each period.

When I first started working, I would claim "1" because I wanted my money now, not later. By claiming "0," you most likely will have a refund at the end of the year because they will be taking the maximum amount of taxes. The higher the number of allowances, the less taken out of your pay each pay period. The W-4 form is filled out upon hire with your job and you can update it at any point in time.

* irs.treasury.gov, 2023

WHEN TO SECURE A PROFESSIONAL

Filing taxes on your own can be manageable, especially when you first start out in your career. There are also many services available that can help you with the process. Through the IRS website, there are free fillable forms that can be used. If needed, seek the advice of a professional tax service such as H&R Block, Clear Tax, CompuTax, TurboTax, or others. Some of these services offer free basic tax software and some may charge a nominal fee, but they will be able to guide you if you have any questions or concerns. If you have a simple tax return, you should be able to file electronically for free.

Whatever you decide for filing taxes, be sure to review your information with your employer and update it each year or as circumstances change. If there is a change before the open enrollment period of insurance and benefits, you have a thirty-day window to let your employer know.

Chapter 9

I CAN . . . SECURE MY FUTURE

Securing your future. It may seem like a lifetime away, but after going through the information in this book, you might be able to somewhat envision it. There have been many things discussed and there is not a one-size-fits-all model. Trust yourself and your abilities to learn more and do more and surround yourself with people who will lift you up even when you are down.

> You are more capable than you think.

There is an abundance of information about finance, but not everything is about investing. My hope is that this will give you some basic understanding of what is useful (while not providing every detail) so that you will continue to research on your own and carve out a path that will work for you now and in your future.

BUILDING WEALTH

Being wealthy and building wealth are two different things. Building wealth is a process that takes time. Being wealthy for some people is to have a nice house and a nice car; to others, it can be traveling where they like, or just being able to pay the bills each month. However you define wealth is up to you, but building wealth over time takes a little bit of discipline, and there are a few key points to consider.

1. Understand your net worth—what is the value of your assets after you take out your debts? If your debts exceed your total assets, then you are said to have a negative net worth.
2. Set financial goals—these should be set for short-term, mid-term, and long-term. A short-term goal might be saving for a weekend getaway, a mid-term goal might be paying off a credit card debt, and a long-term goal could be setting aside enough money to put a down payment on a house. How do you go about setting these goals? Think back to Chapter 1 and setting a budget. Consider what is important to you and if you are able to cut out a dinner once a month. Come up with a short-, mid-, and long-term goal. Look at your income and expenses and adjust as needed.
3. Earn income—we spoke about income from your job. There are three types of income:
   A. Active income from the work that you do.
   B. Passive income, possibly from rental properties or child support payments.
   C. Portfolio income, which includes interest earned on accounts, dividends, or capital gains from selling shares in a mutual fund.

4. Save money automatically by having a portion of your active income directly deposited into a high-yield savings account (paying yourself first).
5. Be mindful of what you are spending—make a list, compare prices, set a limit, or consider delaying a purchase (think it over for a few days).
6. Pay off debt—you can achieve this a few different ways:
   A. The debt avalanche effect says to tackle the high interest first.
   B. The snowball effect focuses on paying the smallest balance first.
   C. You can take out a debt consolidation loan and put it into one payment or complete a balance transfer, which can allow you to transfer from a high interest card to a zero percent or low interest card.
   D. Credit counseling—they may be able to negotiate with lenders on your behalf or lower rates (hopefully, your credit cards will not get to the point where you feel you have no control).
7. Build an emergency fund—use the spreadsheet in the supplemental material to save three, six, or nine months of expenses.
8. Invest your savings into retirement accounts or brokerage accounts.
9. Work with a financial professional (coach, advisor, wealth manager).
10. Protect the wealth that you build by having proper insurance coverage for your job, house, life, etc.
11. Compounding interest.

Recall Chapter 1 and review the table and chart for compounding interest to see how time and compounding interest help to accumulate savings.

Go to the end of the book or youre18nowwhat.com or just use this QR code.

SOCIAL SECURITY

A lot of younger people think that Social Security is not something to think about until much later in life, but as we looked at in Chapters 4 and 8, these are federally mandated taxes to pay that are tracked for as long as you work, which will tie into how much social security you will receive upon retirement. You will need at least ten years of employment (forty credits) to qualify for SSA retirement benefits. You can register an account with the Social Security Administration (SSA) to verify that they have your yearly earnings reported correctly and you can view your estimated retirement benefits. Each year that you work, your income is reported and tracked by SSA so you can see what your potential benefits are at different ages of retirement (between 62 and 70 years old). The longer you wait to apply for retirement benefits, the higher the monthly payment will be.

INVESTMENTS (STOCKS, BONDS, MUTUAL FUNDS, INDEX FUND, AND ETFS)

The financial instruments that are discussed here can all be used to increase wealth. Any time that you invest in stocks, bonds, or other financial instruments, you are taking a risk with your money, but if you look at the long-term investment, you can begin to build wealth. Investopedia and The Motley Fool offer resources for learning about different investments, but we will cover some basics here.

Stocks, also known as equities, are shares of ownership in a company. Investors buy and sell stocks based on their potential to increase in value or to pay dividends. Stock prices change depending on company performance and market demand.

Bonds are issued by governments or corporations as a means of raising money. Bonds are investments in debt, representing a type of fixed-income security. Buying a bond means that an individual lets an entity, usually a corporation or government, borrow their money for a certain period. The entity will then repay the investor, often with interest, in periodic payments. Bonds are less risky than stocks and you make money by holding the bonds until they mature and collect the interest on them. The other profit you can make is by selling the bonds at a higher price than you paid for them.

Mutual Funds are a collection of assets (mutually bought) that invests stocks, bonds, and other securities, so when you purchase a mutual fund, you have a more diversified holding than if you purchased an individual security. Returns on your investment are in the form of an increase in price while you own the fund, income earned from dividends on stocks or interest on bonds, or capital gains (profits) incurred when the fund sells investments.

Index Funds or Exchange-traded funds (ETFs) are investments that follow a benchmark index such as the S&P 500 or the Nasdaq 100. Thc cash you put in is uscd to invcst in all the companies that make up that index, which, again, gives you a more diversified portfolio than buying individual securities. Money made here is also by dividends, interest, and capital gains.

When thinking about retirement income and what you can do immediately for yourself, look at the different Individual Retirement Accounts (IRAs). These are great instruments that you can open on your own and then let them sit until you reach the age of 59½. I know that seems like a lifetime away, but if you can put away some money and forget about it, this is where time and compounding interest will serve you well.

TRADITIONAL IRA AND ROTH IRA

A traditional IRA is an individual retirement account that allows your earnings to grow tax-deferred, meaning that you pay taxes on your investment gains only when you make withdrawals in retirement.

A Roth IRA is an individual retirement account allowing a person to set aside after-tax income up to a specified amount each year. Both earnings on the account and withdrawals from the account after age 59½ are tax-free.

401(K) AND 403(B)

A 401(k) is offered by private, for-profit companies and a 403(b) is offered by nonprofit companies and government organizations. They are both employee-sponsored retirement savings plans that allow employees to contribute a portion of their wages before taxes––some companies will match the employee contribution up to a certain percentage. If you put in 3 percent of your income and your employer puts in 3 percent of your income, you can save money without even thinking about it because it is taken out of your check first.

WILLS, TRUSTS, AND LIFE INSURANCE

A will is a legal document that expresses a person's wishes as to how their property is to be distributed after their death and which person is to manage the property until final distribution. This can be made public, and transfer of assets can take time. A trust is a fiduciary relationship in which one party (the grantor) gives a second party (the trustee) the right to hold the title to property or assets for the benefit of a third party (the beneficiary). A trust takes effect while you are alive, and the assets transfer immediately. It can be more costly, but it stays private.

Life insurance is a way to protect your assets and can be used upon passing to pay off your home or other debts so that your family is protected from covering the costs of a home or debts that they might not be able to afford. Term life insurance is a contract between you and an insurance company for a defined period, typically between ten and thirty years. You purchase $500,000 of term life insurance and pay a set premium each month for the term of the policy.

Upon your passing, your beneficiary will receive the money. Life insurance can also be a way to build wealth. Whole life insurance is a life insurance policy that provides a guaranteed benefit for the entire life of the insured. The monthly premium on a whole life policy is significantly more than a term life policy because it builds cash value, provides permanent coverage if the premiums are paid, builds wealth over the long term, and the cash accumulation in the policy can be accessed at any time if needed.

Whether you are looking at investments or insurance, do your research and see what will work for you. There is not a one-size-fits-all since everyone has different needs at different points in their life. If you decide to meet with a professional, ask for or look up their credentials. Are they a financial consultant or financial planner? An investment

> Life insurance can give some peace of mind.

broker? A wealth advisor? A certified financial planner? Financial planners can assist with creating financial plans, and financial advisors can offer advice on investing money within those plans. Registered financial professionals are licensed sales personnel who work for a broker-dealer firm (buying and selling securities).

The important thing for securing your future is to have the different tax buckets so you can maximize your wealth now and later:

1. Tax Now Bucket—savings accounts, brokerage accounts.
2. Tax Later Bucket—401(k) and 403(b), IRA, pension plans.
3. Tax Advantage Budget—Roth IRA, cash accumulation in an insurance policy.

TAX NOW | TAX LATER | TAX NEVER

MORE TAXES (AND WHY YOU NEED TO KNOW MORE)

We covered some basics of taxes and tax collection, but here we will cover the types of taxes and how to reduce your taxable income.

Income Tax: collected from people who draw an income in the United States. These include wages, salaries, dividends, capital gains, alimony payments, unemployment checks, and even Social Security benefits if a person's income reaches a certain level.

Payroll Tax: withheld by employers and paid directly to the government. The Federal Insurance Contributions Act (FICA) is the largest payroll tax and goes to fund Social Security and Medicare. State and federal unemployment taxes are also paid by employers.

Sales Tax: these are collected at the point of purchase for goods and services and are paid by the end user (consumer). Sales tax can be applied at the federal, state, and local levels.

Property Tax: collected from homeowners based on the assessed value of the property and assessed at the local level. These fund local roads and services such as police, fire, and emergency response personnel.

Taxes are paid by employees each pay period rather than a bulk of money at the end of the year. When a person files their taxes, they will either owe some money because they did not pay enough throughout the year, or they can receive a refund if they have paid too much. So how do you lower your taxable income?

You can contribute to a retirement fund as mentioned earlier, give charitable contributions, have a mortgage interest reduction (an incentive to work toward purchasing a home), or claim a loss where if you have a taxable investment, you can deduct the amount lost from your taxable income. In these scenarios, you will want to hire a tax professional who will know the laws and regulations of filing your return.

You can have standard deductions or itemized deductions for filing—not both. Tax credits are separate from tax deductions and decrease the amount of your taxable income. The child tax credit or child and dependent care credit are examples.

Securing your future involves more than financial security. It is ever-changing, and what you need as a 16- or 18-year-old is not what you need as a 22- or 25-year-old. As you build a life for yourself and start to carve your own path with career choices, personal growth and development, health and wellness, and financial planning, these decisions are constant. What choices you make today can impact your future. The decisions are for the long-term investment in yourself, whether you are investing money, furthering your education, maintaining a healthy lifestyle, or building relationships personally or professionally.

Everyone has a journey and has the option of making choices—some of which can have a significant impact on our lives. The choices you make, the relationships you form, the money you save and invest will be filled with challenges and rewards, but making the commitment to yourself, your goals, and your dreams will give you the security and peace of mind knowing that you put yourself first as you navigate through this wonderful thing we call life.

What are you waiting for—*You're 18! Now What?*

SUPPLEMENTAL MATERIAL

Supplemental materials presented here are also available for downloading from my website, youre18nowwhat.com, or by scanning the QR code that is located throughout the book.

50/30/20 BUDGET

YOUR MONTHLY BUDGET: 50/30/20 RULE	
Sheets 2, 3, 4, and 5 contain the info you need to create a spending plan for yourself going forward. This sheet helps you plan using the 50/30/20 rule. Use the Income section to figure out how much take-home pay you earn per month. Then fill out the expenses that you expect to fall into your Needs, Fun, and Future You buckets below.	
INCOME	
Gross pay listed on paycheck	
Taxes and Social Security per paycheck	
Number of paychecks you get per month	2
Monthly after-tax (take-home) pay	
NEEDS	
Target percentage	50%
"Needs" budget	
Anticipated spending (from details listed below)	
Difference between budget and anticipated spending	
Anticipated "Needs" spending	Monthly cost
Saving for non-monthly "Needs" expenses	
Voluntary payroll deductions (other than 401(k))	
Minimum student loan payment	
Minimum credit card payment	
Minimum car loan payment	
Monthly rent/mortgage	
Transportation (subway, gas, etc.)	
Cell phone bill	
Internet bill	

Groceries	
Water, sewer, trash	
Parking	
Electric	
Car insurance	
FUN	
Target percentage	30%
"Fun" budget	
Anticipated spending (from details listed below)	
Difference between budget and anticipated spending	
Anticipated "Fun" spending	Monthly cost
Saving for non-monthly "Fun" expenses	
Restaurants and delivery	
Drinks	
Entertainment (movies, concerts, etc.)	
Random awesome stuff I want	
Gym membership	
Donations/charitable giving	
Kids' extra stuff they want	
Extra credit card payments	
FUTURE YOU	
Target percentage	20%
"Future You" budget	
Anticipated spending (from details listed below)	
Difference between budget and anticipated spending	
Anticipated "Future You" spending	Monthly cost
401(k) contributions (auto deduct)	

Student loan payment above minimum	
Credit card payment above minimum	
Car loan payment above minimum	
Saving for emergency fund	
Roth IRA	
ALL BUCKETS	
Buckets add up to	100.00%
Total budgeted	
Anticipated spending	
Wiggle room	

CURRENT SPENDING

CURRENT SPENDING			
Look at last month's bank and credit card statements and list each transaction below to get a rough idea of how much you're spending today. (If last month wasn't typical for you, choose one of the last few months that felt typical for you.)			
TRANSACTION	**AMOUNT**	**CATEGORY**	**BUCKET**
Health insurance (deducted from paycheck)		Health and fitness	Needs
Minimum student loan payment		Debt	Needs
Minimum credit card payment		Debt	Needs
Gas (car)		Transportation	Needs
Monthly rent/mortgage		Rent/mortgage	Needs
Parking car		Rent/mortgage	Needs
Water/sewer/trash		Utilities	Needs
Electric		Utilities	Needs
Cell phone		Cell phone service	Needs
Internet		Internet service	Needs
Car insurance		Insurance	Needs
Renter's insurance		Insurance	Needs
Car payment		Transportation	Needs
Mani/Pedi		Entertainment	Fun
Groceries		Groceries	Needs
Streaming services		Entertainment	Fun
Savings		Saving	Future You
Roth IRA		Saving	Future You
(add other categories here)			

TOTAL SPENT:

DEBT INVENTORY

DEBT INVENTORY & AVALANCHE/SNOWBALL PLANNER				
Gather info on all the individual debts you owe today. What are their interest rates, balances, and minimum payments? Then sort by interest rate or current balance to prioritize your debts based on the debt avalanche or snowball methods.				
DEBT NAME	TYPE	INTEREST RATE (sort Z- A for debt avalanche)	CURRENT BALANCE (sort A- Z for debt snowball)	MINIMUM PAYMENT
	Credit card			
	Credit card			
	Credit card			
	Auto loan			
	Federal student loan			
				TOTAL MIN PAYMENT: $0.00

Debt types

- Federal student loan
- Private student loan
- Credit card
- Personal loan
- Auto loan
- Mortgage/rent
- Business loan
- HELOC/Home equity loan

EMERGENCY FUND TARGET

EMERGENCY FUND TARGET CALCULATOR		
Use the calculators below to help you figure out how much take-home pay you earn per month, your emergency fund target, and how much you have left to save until you hit it. Then experiment in the planning space to see what it will take to get there.		
AMOUNT YOU HAVE SAVED TODAY		
TAKE-HOME PAY CALCULATOR		
Gross pay listed on your paycheck		
Taxes and Social Security per paycheck		
Number of paychecks you get per month		
Monthly after-tax (take-home) pay		
TARGET AMOUNT CALCULATOR		
Target	Total	Left to save
1 month take-home pay		
2 months' take-home pay		
3 months' take-home pay		
4 months' take-home pay		
5 months' take-home pay		
6 months' take-home pay		
9 months' take-home pay (self-employed)		
PLANNING SPACE		
If you can afford to save a certain amount each month, how long will it take you to hit your emergency fund target?		
Amount left to save (calculated above)		

Amount you plan to save per month		
Number of months it will take		
If you want to hit your emergency fund target by a certain date, how much do you need to save per month?		
Amount you should save per month		

COVER LETTER

YOUR NAME
Address | Telephone | Email

Date
Recipient
Title
Company
Street Address
City, ST ZIP Code

Dear Recipient:
To get started right away, just tap any placeholder text (such as this) and start typing.

Wondering what to include in your cover letter? It's a good idea to include key points about why you're a great fit for the company and the best choice for the specific job. Of course, don't forget to ask for the interview—but keep it brief! A cover letter shouldn't read like a novel, no matter how great a plot you've got.

Sincerely,
Your Name

RESUME

FIRST NAME
LAST NAME
Address | Phone | Email

Skills Summary
To get started right away, just tap any placeholder text (such as this) and start typing.

Education
Degree/Date of graduation
You might want to include your GPA here and a brief summary of relevant coursework, awards, and honors.

Experience
Name of employer
Job title/Dates of employment
This is the place for a brief summary of your key responsibilities and most stellar accomplishments.

Awards and Acknowledgements
Type of award/award description
Are you president of your fraternity or sorority, head of the condo board, or a team lead for your favorite charity? You're a natural leader—tell it like it is!

CHECKLIST FOR MY IDEAL APARTMENT

CHECKLIST FOR MY IDEAL APARTMENT	
Address: My First Place–what are my needs?	
Number of bedrooms	
Number of bathrooms	
Total square footage	
Office/den/bonus room	
Amount of rent	
Terms of lease (e.g., month-by-month, yearly)	
Location (e.g., near shopping, near bus)	
Pets allowed	
On-site parking	
Utilities included	
Security system	
Heating (e.g., central, forced air)	
Cable	
High-speed internet access	
On-site storage	
On-site laundry facilities	
Fireplace	
Vaulted ceilings	
Floors (e.g., carpet, hardwood, tile)	
View (e.g., water, city, mountain)	
Fitness facility	
Pool	
Club room	
Social events	
On-site management	

NEW APARTMENT TO-DO LIST

- ❏ Water
- ❏ Electric
- ❏ Sewer
- ❏ Natural gas
- ❏ Trash and recycling
- ❏ Cable
- ❏ Internet
- ❏ Secure renter's insurance

Update Address on the Following

- ❏ USPS
- ❏ Employer
- ❏ Driver's license
- ❏ Voter's registration
- ❏ Bank accounts
- ❏ Credit card accounts
- ❏ 401(k), 403(b), stock, and investment accounts
- ❏ Car insurance
- ❏ Medical insurance
- ❏ Any life insurance policies

Apartment Necessities Checklist by Room

If it is not on the list, you can do without it until the budget increases for you—or someone wants to get you a housewarming gift.

Kitchen

- ❏ Plates
- ❏ Bowls

- ❏ Silverware
- ❏ Pots and pans
- ❏ Baking sheets
- ❏ Measuring cups (liquid and dry measure)
- ❏ Blender
- ❏ Toaster and/or toaster oven
- ❏ Coffee pot
- ❏ Mugs and glasses
- ❏ Strainer
- ❏ Can opener
- ❏ Pizza cutter
- ❏ Ice cream scoop
- ❏ Bottle opener and wine opener
- ❏ Trash can
- ❏ Kitchen towels

Living Room and Bedroom

- ❏ TV and TV stand
- ❏ Couch
- ❏ Coffee table
- ❏ Kitchen table and/or bar stools for counter seating
- ❏ Mattress and box spring
- ❏ Sheet set
- ❏ Comforter
- ❏ Pillow
- ❏ Nightstand (one is sufficient)
- ❏ Dresser, desk, and chair (if needed and space allows)

Bathroom and Laundry

- ❏ Toiletries (as mentioned in Chapter 3)

- ❑ Towels (bath, hand, washcloths)
- ❑ Detergent and dryer sheets
- ❑ Hamper (or a basket in the closet will do)
- ❑ Ironing board and iron or steamer

Cleaning Supplies

- ❑ Vacuum
- ❑ Broom and dustpan
- ❑ All-purpose cleaner
- ❑ Shower, tub cleaner, and disinfecting wipes
- ❑ Toilet bowl brush, cleaner, and plunger
- ❑ Glass cleaner and paper towels
- ❑ Dish cleaner and sponge
- ❑ Floor mop and floor cleaner
- ❑ Dust wipe
- ❑ Trash bags

Miscellaneous

- ❑ Bins for pantry, closet, refrigerator, and drawers
- ❑ Hangers
- ❑ Suitcase and garment bag
- ❑ Any supplies needed for your pet if you have one

JOB INTERVIEW CHECKLIST

Interview prep

- ❏ Critique your resume. If it's not had an overhaul for a while, consider getting a professional to give it the magic touch.
- ❏ Review the job description. Make a list of the attributes and skills the company is looking for.
- ❏ Determine how your particular skill set makes you the ideal candidate.
- ❏ Carry out company research. Check their website, employee reviews, and articles in industry-specific publications.
- ❏ Practice with a mock interview. Family and friends will be happy to help.
- ❏ Work out travel logistics. How long will it take you to get there? How will you travel?
- ❏ Consider your interview outfit. Make sure it's job specific.
- ❏ Prepare a list of references with contact details.
- ❏ Create an up-to-date portfolio of job skills and develo-pment.
- ❏ Prepare a list of company specific questions that show you're interested in and have researched the organization.

The day before

- ❏ Ensure your interview outfit is clean and pressed.
- ❏ Pack an emergency kit, including wipes, tissues, comb or brush, umbrella, lint brush, and breath mints.
- ❏ Double-check your route. Do a dry run if necessary.

- ❑ Get all your credentials together, including your portfolio, certifications, industry memberships, driver's license, social security card, and multiple copies of your resume.
- ❑ Get a good night's sleep.

The day of

- ❑ Leave home in plenty of time. Arrive at the interview location 10—15 minutes early.
- ❑ Turn off your cell phone ringer.
- ❑ Do not chew gum, eat, or drink during the interview.
- ❑ Be polite and friendly to reception staff or whoever meets you before the interview.
- ❑ Greet the interviewer by name, shake his or her hand, and introduce yourself.
- ❑ Listen and interact with your interviewers. Smile and be aware of your body language.
- ❑ Answer all questions honestly.
- ❑ Ask your prepared questions that are job and company specific.
- ❑ Avoid talking about salary, benefits, or vacations. This can be done after an offer has been made.
- ❑ Finish the interview by expressing your desire for the job, asking what the next steps will be, and when they plan to make a decision.
- ❑ Ask for business cards from the interviewers to ensure you have contact information.

Post interview

- ❑ Write down key points of the interview as soon as possible.

- ❏ Send a thank-you note to each of the interviewers within 24 hours. This is your chance to show how interested you are and prove, once again, that you're the right candidate for the job.
- ❏ Follow up if you've not heard anything within the time frame discussed.

ACKNOWLEDGMENTS

Wow! Just wow! Where do I begin? What was just a thought years back kept creeping into my head over and over, and I knew I had to follow through and write this book. I have so many people that have supported my work over the years, and I apologize if I am leaving anyone out.

I'll start with the latest group of people that includes Amplify Publishing Group CEO Naren Aryal for believing in my work first, and then having the opportunity to share it with Will Wolfslau and Myles Schrag, who were equally excited and supportive. The entire APG team from start to finish has been instrumental in seeing my work published and I am grateful for their guidance, support, and constructive criticism along the way, and having patience with me as I navigated this journey.

To all my students whom I have encountered over the years—whether in the halls of Delaware Valley University, Bucks County Community College, Delaware County Community College, or

Chestnut Hill College—it has been my pleasure to have taught you, to have learned from you, and to have watched you flourish in your careers. I have enjoyed every moment of being in and out of the classroom with you and still look forward to the personal and professional accomplishments that you share with me.

To my colleagues who I had the opportunity to work alongside, and learn from…thank you. Special thanks to Dr. William J. Cunningham for believing in my book when I first pitched it and never doubting my ability to accomplish anything; Dr. Carolyn Albright for pushing me by saying that I was the right person to write this book; and to Professor Dawn Schramm for being my personal cheerleader and always encouraging me to go forward. Your friendships have meant the world.

Most importantly, I would like to thank my family. I have spent years going to school, writing papers, working, and raising a family. I have always made time for them, but I cherish the time they allowed me to pursue my master's and PhD programs. They always encouraged me to keep going because they knew I would accomplish it. I have always expressed the importance of integrity and work ethic, and I am so incredibly proud of what my children have already accomplished. Stephanie, Brittany, Shaina, and Jake—you are my heart and I hope you know how much you have pushed me to be better and do better.

For my brothers, who drive me crazy at times, I would not trade you for anything in the world. Growing up with Paulie, Vincent, and Danny Boy showed me that I could do anything they could do and maybe even better if I stuck with it. I appreciate how proud they are of me and my accomplishments. I am just as proud of them. For the extended family, I have been inspired by you. Your support of my work throughout my career has been amazing.

For Keith, I have no words. We have been through so much and yet we are still standing. Only you know how much that means to me. ♥

KEY TERMS

401(k): an employee-sponsored retirement savings plan provided by for-profit companies that allows employees to contribute a portion of their wages.

403(b): an employee-sponsored retirement savings plan provided by nonprofit and government employers that allows employees to contribute a portion of their wages.

Amortization: the process of repaying debt in regular installments over a specified period of time.

Annuities: provide insurance against the risk of outliving your money after you stop working.

Asset: an item with economic value that an entity owns ("current assets" or "liquid assets" are assets that owners can easily convert to cash, typically within a year).

Beneficiary: the person or entity that you legally designate to receive the benefits from your financial products.

Bonds: investments in debt, representing a type of fixed-income securities.

Budget: a financial plan to determine spending habits over a particular period, used to compare how much money you spend and how much money you earn.

Checking account: designed to provide quick access to your money for daily transactions, paying bills, or buying products.

Compound interest: the amount of interest earned on a loan or deposit based on the initial amount plus the interest accumulated over time.

Credit: a contractual agreement in which a lender loans money to a borrower with the intent that the borrower will repay it later.

Credit bureau: data collectors who receive information from lenders and creditors and review the information for creditworthiness.

Credit card: a loan in the form of a plastic card with an account number and name on it, issued by a financial institution.

Credit limit: the amount that can be charged on the credit card to purchase goods and services, or the cash advance that can be obtained.

Credit score (FICO score): a three-digit number that measure an individual's trustworthiness (or creditworthiness) to pay back a loan or debt.

Debit card: linked to your checking account so that you can process daily transactions without using cash (the money is taken out almost immediately). You can also use your debit card to access cash via ATMs (automated teller machines).

Debt: something that is owed or due, usually money.

Deductions (tax): an item or expense that can reduce the taxes a person owes in a given year.

Expenses: the costs of operating a household or business (rent, utilities, etc.).

Grantor: the entity that establishes a trust and legally transfers control of those assets to a trustee, who manages it for one or more beneficiaries.

Income: the amount of money received, usually on a regular basis, for work or through investments.

Inflation: overall increase in the price of goods and services over time.

Interest: the amount that individuals pay when borrowing money.

Interest rate: a portion of a loan that is expressed as an annual or monthly percentage of the outstanding loan amount.

Investment: an allocation of money with the expectation of a profit or material benefit in return.

Liability: a debt or amount of money that an entity owes to another entity (bank loans, credit card debts).

Loan: a sum of money or an item that one entity lets another entity borrow.

Medicaid: government program that provides insurance for adults and children with limited income and resources.

Medicare: government health insurance program for people over the age of 65 or certain younger people with disabilities

Money market fund: used by investors who want to protect rather than grow their savings but still aim to earn some interest.

Mortgage: a loan used to buy property.

Mutual fund: a professionally managed investment program funded by shareholders that trade in diversified holding.

Pension: a regular payment made during a person's retirement from an investment fund to which that person or their employer has contributed during their working life.

Rent: a regular payment to a landowner for the use of property or land.

Roth IRA: an individual retirement account allowing a person to set aside after-tax income up to a specified amount each year.

Salary: a fixed regular payment from employer to employee, typically paid on a monthly or biweekly basis but often expressed as an annual amount.

Savings account: where money is kept for saving or future use.

Securities: tradable financial instruments used to raise capital in private and public markets.

Stocks: also called "equities"—portions or shares of ownership in a company.

Taxes: fees paid by individuals and businesses to governments, which fund government spending and public programs (national defense, police and firefighters, community development, etc.).

Term life insurance: a life insurance policy for a defined period, typically between ten and thirty years, that will pay a death benefit.

Traditional IRA: an individual retirement account that allows your earnings to grow tax deferred.

Trust: a fiduciary relationship in which one party (the grantor) gives a second party (the trustee) the right to hold the title to property or assets for the benefit of a third party (the beneficiary).

Unemployment insurance: a monetary benefit to a person who has recently lost their job via no fault of their own (lay-off, downsizing).

Whole life insurance: a life insurance policy that builds cash value, provides permanent coverage as long as the premiums are paid, and can build wealth over the long-term.

Will: a legal document that expresses a person's wishes as to how their property is to be distributed after their death and which person is to manage the property until final distribution.

Workers compensation insurance: coverage purchased by the employer or business that provides benefits for job-related employee injuries.

REFERENCES

Apartments.com (2023). https://www.apartments.com/rent-affordability-calculator/

Brown, T., Apenteng, B.A., & Opoku, S.T. (2022). Factors associated with cost conversations in oral health care settings. *Journal of the American Dental Association, 153*(9), 829–838. https://doi.org/10.1016/j.adaj.2022.04.003.

Del Vecchio, J., & Jacobs, T. (2016). *Rule of 72: How to compound your money and uncover hidden stock profits.* Sovereign Society.

Internal Revenue Service (2023). https://www.irs.gov

National Institutes of Health (2023). https://www.ncbi.nlm.nih.gov

Progressive Home Renters (2021). https://www.progressive.com/answers/average-renters-insurance-cost/

SHRM.org (2023). https://www.shrm.org/ResourcesAndTools/hr-topics/benefits/Pages/default.aspx

Social Security Administration (2023). https://www.ssa.gov

Studentaid.gov (2023). https://studentaid.gov/understand-aid/types/loans/subsidized-unsubsidized

The Book of Inside Information: Money, Health, Shopping, Taxes, Marriage, Home, Investments, Fitness, Car, Travel, Collecting Retirement, Success, Education (1993). Boardroom Classics.

US Citizen and Immigration Services (2023). https://www.uscis.gov

US Department of Labor (2023). https://www.dol.gov

ABOUT THE AUTHOR

Dr. Catherine Gilstein, MBA, PhD, has been teaching business courses at the college level for the past ten years. She has also spent twenty-plus years in the financial services industry and conducted her dissertation research on women in STEM (science, technology, engineering, and math) and their career development. Catherine is committed to her students. She has earned a reputation for integrity and true concern, and cares about education and economic empowerment. She enjoys traveling and spending time with her family, reading on the beach, and writing in her spare time. *You're 18! Now What?* is her first book.

in /CATHERINE-GILSTEIN

youre18nowwhat.com